THE CREATIVE CLASSROOM

THE CREATIVE CLASSROOM

Innovative Teaching for 21st-Century Learners

KEITH SAWYER

Foreword by Tony Wagner

TEACHERS COLLEGE PRESS

TEACHERS COLLEGE | COLUMBIA UNIVERSITY

NEW YORK AND LONDON

Published by Teachers College Press, 1234 Amsterdam Avenue, New York, NY
10027

Front cover images: Chair by Chris Ryan, balloons by spfdigital, both via iStock by
Getty Images.

Library of Congress Cataloging-in-Publication Data

Names: Sawyer, R. Keith (Robert Keith) author.
Title: The creative classroom : innovative teaching for 21st-century
    learners / R. Keith Sawyer ; Foreword by Tony Wagner.
Description: New York, NY : Teachers College Press, [2019] | Includes
    bibliographical references and index.
Identifiers: LCCN 2019023507 (print) | LCCN 2019023508 (ebook) | ISBN
    9780807761212 (paperback) | ISBN 9780807763049 (hardback) | ISBN
    9780807777633 (ebook)
Subjects: LCSH: Creative teaching. | Creative ability in children. |
    Student-centered learning. | Classroom environment.
Classification: LCC LB1025.3 .S29 2019 (print) | LCC LB1025.3 (ebook) |
    DDC 371.102—dc23
LC record available at https://lccn.loc.gov/2019023507
LC ebook record available at https://lccn.loc.gov/2019023508

ISBN 978-0-8077-6121-2 (paper)
ISBN 978-0-8077-6304-9 (hardcover)
ISBN 978-0-8077-7763-3 (ebook)

Printed on acid-free paper
Manufactured in the United States of America

Contents

Foreword

For the first half of the 20th century, when most people earned their living on farms and in factories, physical strength and manual dexterity were competitive advantages. Then came what Peter Drucker (1969) termed "the knowledge economy." In this new era, brains mattered more than brawn because the ability to access and analyze information became a key driver of economic growth. The more you knew and the more facile you were with your knowledge, the greater the competitive advantage. As a result, for the past 50 years our education systems have focused on ensuring that students acquire and retain massive amounts of information.

But we no longer live in a knowledge economy. The world no longer cares how much you know, because Google knows everything. There is no longer a competitive advantage in knowing more than the person next to you because what the world cares most about is not what you know, but what you can do with what you know. One's competitive advantage today comes from the ability to bring new possibilities to life or to solve problems creatively—in other words, to innovate. Of course, you need knowledge to accomplish these things. It is necessary, but not sufficient. In the innovation era, knowledge still matters, but skills matter more, and motivation and dispositions matter most.

From elementary schools through graduate schools, our education systems have not begun to adapt to this new reality. At every level and in every course, the primary focuses are on content knowledge acquisition. Rarely do students have opportunities to apply their knowledge, to hone their skills, to pursue their own interests. As human beings, we are born curious, creative, imaginative. The average 5-year-old asks 100 questions a day, and most kindergartners think of themselves as artists. But by the time most kids reach the age of 12 or so, they are far more preoccupied with getting the right answers on tests than they are on continuing to ask their own questions, and fewer think of themselves as creative.

The price our students pay for this kind of education is very high and rarely discussed. We are raising generations of students who are obsessed with getting good grades and scoring well on tests—doing everything they think they need to do to get into a name-brand college so they can have a name-brand job and live happily ever after. These kids are terrified of making a single mistake and getting less than an A. In desperate pursuit of trying to market themselves and be the perfect kid for the right college, they lose sight of who they really are, what their questions are, what they're curious about.

Meanwhile, the kids who don't compete because they'd rather work with their hands or don't think they're smart enough feel like losers. Twenty percent of our students don't complete high school. An additional 30% graduate from high school and go on to minimum-wage jobs. Of the approximately 70% of high school graduates who enroll in college, nearly half drop out before they complete any degree, often having acquired enormous debt along the way. Lacking skills or preparation for a trade, most of them can only manage to find minimum-wage jobs.

But what about the kids who manage to graduate from a 4-year college or university and then head off into the labor market? Having attended schools where acquiring knowledge mattered most, how well are they faring in the innovation era? A growing body of evidence suggests that, in fact, the majority of our college graduates are stunningly ill prepared for the jobs of the present and even less so for the jobs of the future, when computers and AI will have taken over virtually all routine work.

A couple of examples tell the story. Back in the early days of Google, when everyone still thought we had a knowledge economy, the fledgling company sought to hire the smartest people in the world, so they only hired kids with Ivy League degrees and only interviewed those who had the highest test scores and GPAs. Then along came Laszlo Bock. As senior vice president of people operations at Google, he analyzed all of the data related to hiring and job performance and discovered that the indices they had been using like GPAs and test scores were "worthless." Today, Google no longer asks for test scores or college transcripts. They don't care if you went to college, and 15% of their new hires in certain departments do not have a college degree. They now use multiple structured interviews to make hiring decisions.

When I learned this, I thought that perhaps Google was just an anomaly. Then several years ago, I was invited by Deloitte to speak to business leaders in Ho Chi Minh City. Prior to my presentation, I had lunch with their CEO, who knew of my affiliation at the time to Harvard. She had a bit of fun with that by telling me, "You know, we used to hire the best students from the best universities, but it turned out that they did not work out so well. Now, we put prospective new hires through a summer-long boot camp to see how they solve problems collaboratively, and then we decide whether or not to offer them a job."

For college graduates who do not know how to solve problems collaboratively and who lack other essential skills required to succeed in the innovation era, it is hardly the "full employment economy" that everyone touts these days. According to a recent article in the *Wall Street Journal* (Korn,

2018), 43% of college graduates ages 25 to 29 are either unemployed or underemployed. Many are living at home and likely to default on their college loan debts. The mantra of policymakers for the last decade has been to ensure that all kids graduate from high school "college ready." The assumption is that the more education a student acquires, the better positioned they are to succeed. But the reality is that students today need a different kind of education, not necessarily more education.

Teaching students to be creative is no longer something that is "nice to have." It is a must-have. It is the only set of skills and dispositions that will give students a meaningful competitive advantage in the innovation era. Creative problem-solving skills are equally important for active and informed citizenship in our democracy. Students who learn to stay curious and to pursue their own interests are far more likely to use their leisure for creative activities rather than the pursuit of forms of passive consumption.

But can creativity be taught? And if so, then how? Keith Sawyer has spent most of his professional life considering these questions. This book provides both a theoretical rationale and a hands-on guide to teachers who want to introduce more creativity into their classroom. He understands that students need knowledge in order to create, but it has to be what he calls "creative knowledge"—knowledge that is rooted in a deep understanding. He also makes an important contribution to 21st-century pedagogy in his description of "guided improvisation." He explains that creativity needs prompts and guardrails and cannot happen in a vacuum.

My advice to teachers: Try it! Try the approaches that Sawyer outlines in this clear and concise book. In my experience, both teachers and students feel far more engaged and fulfilled in creative classrooms. Students who are taught by these new methods will also be far better prepared for their future.

Tony Wagner
Cambridge, MA

REFERENCES

Drucker, P. (1969). *The age of discontinuity.* New York, NY: Harper & Row.
Korn, M. (2018, October 26). Some 43% of college grads are underemployed in first job. *The Wall Street Journal.* Retrieved from www.wsj.com/articles/study-offers-new-hope-for-english-majors-1540546200

Acknowledgments

My first and most important thanks is to Emily Spangler, my editor at Teachers College Press. Emily was wonderful. We started with a shared belief that research could help teachers teach for creativity. Our early conversations helped me conceptualize the book and write the book proposal. About halfway through my writing process, Emily read a very drafty, early manuscript, and her insightful comments helped me choose the best way forward. When I submitted the near-final manuscript, she read it closely again and provided specific suggestions for how to refine and focus the text.

The production team at Teachers College Press, including Lori Tate, Karl Nyberg, and copyeditor Kathy Caveney, did a fantastic job. They guided the project through the many steps it takes to turn a manuscript into book. Joy Mizan is a great publicist, and you probably heard about this book because of her good work!

I am grateful to the 14 students in my Fall 2018 doctoral seminar, Introduction to the Learning Sciences, who read early chapter drafts and provided substantial and valuable suggestions: Andrew Chin, Bogeum Choi, Samantha Cullum, Daniel Dinkins, Alex Hoppe, Matthew Hutchinson, Sarah Lasseter, Leah Metcalf, Carrie Moore, Laura Sjoquist, Kristy Stout, Kelsey Van Dyke, Zhijun Wen, and Jian Xiao.

In my 20 years of teaching college students, it took me a lot of trial and error to teach effectively with guided improvisation. In my first few years I learned as much from my students as they did from me. They were learning a new way of learning, just as I was learning a new way of teaching. I owe a lot to those students who provided frank and honest feedback on how I could better manage the teaching paradox.

I would like to thank Musette and Allen Morgan for establishing The Morgan Distinguished Professorship in Educational Innovations Fund which supported my work on this book. This generous gift supported my writing during the summer of 2018.

CHAPTER 1

Introduction

Here are two questions that I ask my college students every semester. After you answer each question, I'll share their answers with you. You might be surprised!

First, think back through your education in high school and college:

Did you ever get an A in a class, and then a month later, you'd forgotten everything you'd learned?

When I ask this question in my classes, all of the students raise their hands. They do it quickly, without hesitation. They look around, and they see everyone else's hands in the air. They smile knowingly; they're not surprised. They think this is just the way school is. In fact, they're right; studies repeatedly show that students, even the best students, don't retain what they learn in school.

Here is the second question:

Did you ever get an A in a class, but you didn't understand anything you were learning?

When I ask the second question, students are quiet at first. They look around the class nervously. A few tentatively start to raise their hands. Several other hands slowly go up. As each student realizes that they're not the only one, almost all of them gradually raise their hands. This time, they seem surprised. Many students think that they were the only one who didn't understand the material, and they're embarrassed to admit it. I quickly reassure them that I expected everyone's hands to go up. That's because researchers have found that in today's schools, even the students who do well on tests often don't understand the material.

All of us have experienced wonderful classes and great teachers. We learned a lot of valuable things that we still remember. But the raised hands—and possibly your own answers—show that everyone has had at least one class that was taught ineffectively. In fact, you probably had a lot of classes like this because many schools use an ineffective pedagogy that I call *instructionism*. In instructionism, the teacher "instructs" the students, telling

1

them what she wants them to learn. The students do their best to memorize that knowledge, and later they demonstrate that they've "learned" by taking a test. But when students are taught with instructionism, they learn only superficial facts and procedures (P. C. Brown, Roediger, & McDaniel, 2014). Students in these classrooms use only the simplest levels of cognitive processing as they learn (Chen & Yang, 2019; Lamb, 2003; Thomas, 2000). As a result, they learn what I call *shallow knowledge*. Good students can remember shallow knowledge just long enough to do well on the test, but they almost all forget it right after the test is over.

I know my students are going to raise their hands when I ask these two questions; they always do. That's why I'm pretty sure that you answered "yes" to both questions. But even though I'm not surprised, I never stop being sad. It's bad enough that students don't remember and don't understand what they learn. But what concerns me most is that students don't learn in ways that prepare them to be creative.

You can't be creative with shallow knowledge. If we only teach shallow knowledge in science, or history, or math, then our students won't be prepared to be creative in those subjects. All of our research shows that it's not enough to teach "creativity" as a general ability, if at the same time you keep teaching shallow knowledge in all of the subjects. The best way to teach creativity is to teach *creative knowledge* in all subjects. When you learn creative knowledge, you understand what you're learning. Creative knowledge is adaptable; you can apply it to new situations and use it outside of school. When you're given a problem you haven't seen before, creative knowledge prepares you to approach it using a deeper understanding of the material. Learning scientists know how to teach for creative knowledge in every subject, and my goal in this book is to help you use this research to design your own creative classroom (e.g., Bransford, Brown, & Cocking, 2000; Darling-Hammond et al., 2008; Mayer & Alexander, 2011; Pellegrino & Hilton, 2012; Sawyer, 2014).

When I ask my students the two questions presented above, their answers make it painfully obvious that in instructionist classrooms, even the best students don't learn for understanding. Learning sciences research confirms that this isn't unique to my classes or to my two questions. For example, take a look at these two test items, both of which can be solved using a fairly straightforward application of the Pythagorean theorem (items quoted by Wiggins & McTighe, 2005, p. 42).

From the New York State Regents Exam:
To get from his high school to his home, Jamal travels 5.0 miles east and then 4.0 miles north. When Sheila goes to her home from the same high school, she travels 8.0 miles east and 2.0 miles south. What is the measure of the shortest distance, to the nearest tenth of a mile, between Jamal's home and Sheila's home? (The use of the accompanying grid is optional.)

From the National Assessment of Educational Progress (NAEP) 12th-grade mathematics test:
What is the distance between the points (2,10) and (-4, 2) in the xy plane? The five multiple-choice options include: 6, 8, 10, 14, and 18.

The students who take these tests have all been taught the Pythagorean theorem. Many of them got an A grade on that material. So it's shocking that only about 30% of test takers got the right answer. That's horrible, especially when you realize that even if everyone just picked at random from among the five possible answers, 20% would get it right! A similar question appears on the Massachusetts Comprehensive Assessment System (MCAS) 10th-grade math test, with similarly bad results. More students got this question wrong than any other question on the MCAS test. Even though the above questions can be easily solved using the theorem, they're posed in a slightly different way than students learned in class. The students had memorized the formula, but only in a shallow way. They might be able use their shallow knowledge to solve the problems they were given in the classroom, but on the Regents, NAEP, and MCAS tests they weren't given the same simple problems they had in class (Wiggins & McTighe, 2005, pp. 42–43).

Most students in the United States can't do these problems, even though every state standard includes the Pythagorean theorem as an important learning outcome in math. The problem is that the formula $x^2 + y^2 = z^2$ is taught as a rule that you use on a certain type of classroom problem, a rule that you use over and over to solve 30 identical problems on a worksheet. But if you remove just a few simple cues—even though they don't change the underlying structure of the problem—students can't do it. It's because the students didn't understand what they were learning.

Performance on the NAEP shows that students, in general, can do low-level shallow-knowledge tasks, but almost all of them are weak in higher-order understanding. And it's not only in math; students perform just as badly when they're tested on social studies topics—like honor, manifest destiny, immigration—or science topics, like the water cycle (Wiggins & McTighe, 2005, pp. 43–45).

&

In 1900, about 95% of jobs were low-skilled and required workers to follow simple procedures that were designed by others. Today, less than 10% of jobs are like this. We live in a creative age, and any activity that doesn't involve creativity will soon be automated. Working-class factory jobs have been taken over by computers and robots. With recent advances in artificial intelligence (AI), many white-collar jobs will be automated next (see, e.g., Partnership for 21st Century Skills, 2019; Pink, 2005; Trilling & Fadel, 2009; Wagner, 2012a).[1]

If we're only teaching our students shallow knowledge, then we're wasting their time and ours. Our students need creative classrooms, not old-fashioned instructionist classrooms that fill our students' heads with shallow knowledge. In Chapter 3 I describe a research-based pedagogy that I call *guided improvisation* .[2] The pedagogy is *improvisational* because teachers give students freedom to explore the subject and create their own understandings. The learning benefits of free and playful exploration are supported by constructivist research; this is the essence of progressive education movements from Maria Montessori to John Dewey. Many critics have attacked these progressive, constructivist approaches, claiming that they ignore standards, curricular goals, and assessments. Creative education is often associated with unconstrained exploration and personal expression, but I'll show that students learn creative knowledge more effectively if their classroom activities are constrained and structured (Sawyer, 2011a). Improvisational knowledge construction must be *guided* so that each student's learning pathway leads to important subject-area learning outcomes, and the class reaches its curricular goals.

This book shows how to develop curricula, lesson plans, and instructional strategies that provide students with the freedom they need to construct their own knowledge, guided so that they learn the subject-area knowledge that's required by state and national standards. I hope that all schools become places where students learn creative knowledge in every subject, instead of the shallow knowledge of instructionism.

In creative classrooms students experiment with their developing knowledge. As they experiment, they learn how to apply what they learn to the next unit's information. They learn how to use their knowledge to approach new challenges. They learn how to think beyond the information they're given. They learn to approach new problems and find creative solutions. Creative knowledge is deep, connected, and adaptable.

Guided improvisation isn't easy, especially for beginning teachers. It's hard to balance structure and freedom. You'll face the *teaching paradox*: How can you give students the freedom advocated by progressive educators for almost a century, the freedom that's needed for creative learning, and at the same time guide their learning improvisations with structures? In Chapter 4 I provide practical advice for how teachers can address the teaching paradox.

In every chapter I'll tell stories about schools that are filled with creative classrooms. I'll introduce you to teachers who guide their students' learning improvisations. My examples come from rural and urban schools, and affluent suburban districts and inner cities. Guided improvisation can work with all populations and neighborhoods. In fact, there's some evidence that it's even more effective with students who haven't done well in traditional schools. All of these schools have been wildly successful. Student learning outcomes are high, both on new measures for creative knowledge, but also—perhaps surprisingly—on the shallow knowledge that they were supposed to learn better through instructionism.

⁊

Most of us spent our whole lives in instructionist schools, so it's not surprising that most people think this is just the way schools are. When you ask someone to define *learning*, they almost always describe instructionism. For example, they say that you learn by listening to the teacher. They describe sitting in front of all-knowing teachers who tell them what they need to know. I recently read a fascinating study in which researchers asked children to draw pictures of a teacher. Almost all of the children drew a woman standing in front of a blackboard or desk, pointing at the board or lecturing to the class (Weber & Mitchell, 1995).

Many preservice teachers start their programs with instructionist views of teaching (Donaldson, 2018; Patrick & Pintrich, 2001; Richardson, 1996; Wideen, Mayer-Smith, & Moon, 1998). When psychologist Stacy DeZutter (2008) asked preservice and practicing teachers to draw sketches of a teacher, their sketches were no different from the children's! As you read this book, I hope that you'll reflect on your own assumptions about teaching. After all, you've experienced a lifetime of instructionist teaching, just like my college students. My goal is to show you a new and better way of teaching: guided improvisation for creative knowledge.

In Chapter 2 I draw on the latest research in learning and in creativity to describe what creative knowledge looks like.

- Creative knowledge is *deep knowledge*—a conceptual understanding of the basic principles and theories of the subject that underlies and provides context to shallow knowledge.
- Creative knowledge is *big knowledge*—a broad understanding of a subject. It brings together a lot of different shallow knowledge in a conceptual system, an explanatory framework, a rich and elaborated model.
- Creative knowledge is *connected knowledge*—each piece of small knowledge is linked to many others, in the same subject and also across disciplines, in a network of related knowledge.

Shallow knowledge, no matter how much of it students learn, doesn't support creativity. It's almost impossible for a student to learn how to be creative in an instructionist classroom. In creative classrooms, in contrast, students learn creative knowledge in every subject, and they're prepared to go beyond what they've learned.

Shallow knowledge has its uses. In the distant past most students didn't have access to books or to a library. Without communication technology—like phones or the Internet—it wasn't always easy to find someone else who knew the information you needed, so you had to know it yourself. Memorizing information was a large part of being educated. But today, memorizing shallow knowledge is just about worthless. With today's Internet, everything that can be memorized is a quick search away. In 2002 five exabytes of new information was created, more than 500,000 times the print collection of the Library of Congress. From 1999 to 2002 the new information produced was about the same as all of the information produced by humankind up to 1999. Today, the amount of technical information doubles every 2 years (McCain, Jukes, & Crockett, 2010; Varian & Lyman, 2003).

Today's mission for teachers is to prepare students to thrive in the 21st century. But we can't ask teachers to do it alone. Teaching with guided improvisation is hard, and teachers need to be supported by a learning community that includes school leaders and parents. Almost everything about schools for creativity is different: culture, leadership, assessments, and structures. In Chapter 5 I describe the new kind of schools that teachers need to support them in the important task of teaching for creativity.

TEACHING WITH GUIDED IMPROVISATION

To realize their creative potential, students need to learn for creative knowledge in each subject. Every class needs to be taught for creative learning outcomes. That's because creative ability is *domain-specific*. To be creative in a subject, you need creative knowledge in that subject (cf. Pellegrino & Hilton, 2012, on "deeper learning"). For example, learning to create in art doesn't increase a student's creativity in math (Hetland & Winner, 2004). Learning to be creative in math doesn't increase a student's creativity in biology. That's why our students need creative classrooms in every subject.

There's a lot of talk today about 21st-century skills, including critical thinking, communication skills, and creativity. Politicians, business leaders, and even parents are asking schools to teach for creativity. Some school leaders respond by adding a creativity course or more arts courses. I'm an advocate of arts education, but if a school remains instructionist at the core, arts education alone can't solve the problem. Trying to teach creativity in an instructionist school is like using a Band-Aid to fix a broken leg. We have to attack the root of the problem: We have to transform schools into creative learning organizations where students and teachers create knowledge, every day and in every subject.

Shallow knowledge is often defended by people who argue that it's aligned with mandatory high-stakes tests. But students who are taught for creative knowledge do just as well, if not better, on today's tests of shallow knowledge. In creative classrooms students learn more, and they learn it

---

KILL THE LECTURE!

In 2002 a new college was created from the ground up: Olin College of Engineering, in Needham, Massachusetts (www.olin.edu; also see Wagner, 2012a, Chapter 5). Olin has a radical vision for engineering education: Abolish the instructionism of large lecture halls and teach for creative knowledge through guided improvisation. Olin is an incredible success story; engineering educators from all over the country are visiting to see how they do it. Olin's founders realized that in most colleges, engineers weren't learning creative knowledge. Students sat in lectures where they memorized decontextualized facts. Before the college opened, the newly hired faculty had to retrain themselves to teach with guided improvisation. They developed a hands-on, interdisciplinary approach, aligned with the creativity of engineering practice. Guided improvisation is now being increasingly adopted by engineering schools across the U.S. To help these innovative engineering schools teach for creativity, Purdue University created the first-ever School of Engineering Education in 2004 (engineering.purdue.edu/ENE).

---

better. But because today's tests only measure shallow knowledge, the dramatic failings of instructionism aren't always visible. When students are assessed with these tests, they can get As even when they don't learn for retention, even when they don't understand the material, and even though they can't be creative with what they've learned.

My good news is that you don't have to make a choice between teaching for creativity and teaching for subject-area knowledge. Guided improvisation leads to creative knowledge, and it also results in better subject-area knowledge. When students learn creative knowledge, they also learn shallow knowledge better (Mayer, 2010; Pellegrino & Hilton, 2012). They retain it better, they understand it better, and they can adapt it to new problems. In Chapter 5 I describe new assessments that reveal creative knowledge, and I describe how schools can start using these assessments to support creative learning.

Throughout this book, I give examples of schools that have succeeded with creative classrooms—primary schools, secondary schools, and colleges. I also give examples of creative learning outside of school, in places like makerspaces and interactive science centers, where learners have a lot of room to improvise. These environments have much less structure than schools could ever have. But even so, I think that teachers can learn a lot from these innovative environments. They show us the potential of guided improvisation for creative learning. Teachers can adopt some of the improvisational features of informal learning environments, while adding the structure needed to guide student activities toward required subject-area learning outcomes.

FACING THE TEACHING PARADOX

Teachers face constraints that are often mandated by law, district administration, or state and federal guidelines. They limit what teachers can do in classrooms (Olson, 2003). How can anyone teach with guided improvisation in the face of so many structures? This isn't a new problem; there has always been a tension between teacher professional autonomy and institutional constraints (e.g., Cochrane-Smith & Lytle, 1999; Darling-Hammond, 1997; Ingersoll, 2003). The tension exists within instructionist classrooms, too, but in creative classrooms, dealing with structures is significantly more challenging—because structure and improvisation are always in tension. I call this the teaching paradox, and in Chapter 4, I'll show you how to develop lesson plans and instructional strategies that foster creative learning, even in the presence of constraints.

Many schools have successfully taken on this challenge, like the York School in Monterey, California (Creason, 2017). The York School is a strong advocate of guided improvisation for learning and creativity. The whole team—teachers and school leaders—realize that what they're doing is very different from the instructionism that you find in most schools. The school's leaders have learned that when a new teacher joins the staff, they often start out using instructionist techniques. For many new hires, guided improvisation can seem like "wishy-washy land," according to Kevin Brookhouser, Director of Technology at the York School. These new teachers don't stick with instructionism because they're stubborn or incapable of change. After all, Brookhouser has hired them because they're great teachers. They truly want their students to learn, and they teach that way because they believe it's best for their students. Brookhouser understands this: "Teachers really want to do the right thing, and it's easy to recognize that you're doing the right thing when you're following a structured curriculum, you know, pulling out a box of the curriculum, and you got these worksheets and you got these quizzes, and you'll be like 'I know I'm doing my job. I'm doing the right thing.'" Teachers who have been through this personal and professional transformation are honest: it's not easy. The York School supports teachers through an onboarding process that mentors them in guided improvisation.

Lynn Stein, a professor at Olin College of Engineering, says "You have to have a different notion of yourself and your role [as a teacher]. Being the 'sage on the stage' is problematic when you're trying to encourage intrinsic motivation and encourage students to have ownership of their learning. . . . It's hard to make the shift to being the 'guide on the side,' though. Giving up control is a huge issue for many teachers who are used to the old way" (Wagner, 2012a, p. 161). Another Olin professor, materials scientist Jon Stolk, said: "Traditional classrooms are all about instructor control. You tell students what's important to learn and why, and then you evaluate them. . . . Faculties over the ages have based their sense of competence on

> ## THE CREATIVE TEACHER'S BILL OF RIGHTS
>
> - You have the right to question any policies or instructions that influence your ability to teach and your students' ability to learn.
> - You have the right to the freedom necessary to choose the best strategies to meet your students' needs, and to adapt the assigned lesson plans to your classroom.
> - You have the right to an open curriculum that allows for choice and adaptability in your classroom.
> - You have the right to take risks and not be chastised if some of these risks seem to fail.
> - You have the right to a work environment where sharing ideas and offering help is the norm.
> - You have the right to be treated as the professional you are.
>
> (Schrek, 2009, p. 65)

what they know versus how they facilitate learning. It's a huge shift. It took me many years" (Wagner, 2012a, pp. 162–163).

Now that Lynn and Jon have learned this new way of teaching, they say they would never go back. Teachers at York say the same. Guided improvisation is fulfilling and motivating. You can see how much your students are learning. You believe in what you're doing. Once you learn how to teach creative knowledge with guided improvisation, you'll never return to instructionism.

THE CREATIVE TEACHERS OF THE FUTURE

There are three ways you can work for change in education. One is to support schools from the outside—perhaps by developing new educational software, or by joining the local school board. In my case, I chose to become a learning sciences researcher and to study the creative classrooms where the most effective learning happens. A second way to work toward change is to give up on the public schools of today and to start all over from scratch. These educational reformers think today's schools are hopeless bureaucracies that will never change. Instead, they try to innovate outside of traditional schools, with charters or private schools, or with new delivery methods enabled by the Internet.

This book is for people who have chosen the third path: for the teachers who have chosen to change schools from the inside, in their own creative classrooms. For the teachers who accept the challenge to teach for creativity, one day and one student at a time. For the teachers who have dedicated their lives to building the creative classrooms we need in the 21st century.

NOTES

1. There have been many studies of these changes, and their implications for teaching and schooling, including Bell (1973); Drucker (1994); Florida (2002); Friedman (2005); and The Secretary's Commission on Achieving Necessary Skills (SCANS) (1991).

2. In earlier publications, I called this pedagogy "disciplined improvisation" (Sawyer, 2004a, 2004b, 2011b). For this book, I chose to rename this "guided improvisation" because I've learned that for many readers, the word "disciplined" had connotations of teacher authority. After all, discipline is a synonym for punish. Some other readers have said that it sounded like I was referring to the school subjects, as in the "discipline" of physics.

CHAPTER 2

Teaching Creative Knowledge

Since I received my PhD in psychology in 1994, I've devoted my career to the study of creativity and learning. Since then our knowledge has grown dramatically. Researchers now know a lot about how people learn to be creative. But this research hasn't been available to teachers, and that's why I wrote this book. Most teacher education programs don't mention creativity at all, and most education textbooks don't tell teachers how to foster creativity (DeZutter, 2008; Mack, 1987). So it's not surprising that very few teachers have learned to use creative teaching techniques (Schacter, Thum, & Zifkin, 2006).

I love to share my research, and that's why I give invited talks and key-notes on creativity and learning around the United States. In conversations before and after my talks, I've learned that many people come to the talk with a few common misconceptions about creativity. Some of these beliefs are harmless, like the (false) belief that creativity takes place in the right brain, or the (misleading) belief that children are naturally creative until school beats it out of them (more on that at the end of this chapter). But the misconceptions that worry me the most are the ones that make it seem like creativity is out of our reach. Some people have heard that creativity is re-served for gifted geniuses. Others think that creativity is reserved for people who are mentally ill, or that creativity requires that you be a bit eccentric, or that creative people reject norms and stand outside of society. If this were what creativity is, there would be no way to teach it. However, researchers now know that none of these beliefs are true (Sawyer, 2012). Creativity isn't genetic; it isn't reserved for geniuses or the mentally ill; and it's not a personality trait that only a few artsy people have.

I've also heard a few people say that the most radical new ideas in a field come from people who don't know that much about the field—newcomers or dilettantes. They suggest that knowledge constrains your thought and keeps you from thinking outside the box. If so, then it should be even more of a problem for senior leaders and experts in a field; they would be so in-vested in the status quo that they would be likely to reject any ideas that are truly transformative. In other words, more knowledge equals less creativity. And if so, the more effectively you teach someone, the less creative they will be. Isn't that a horrifying thought for teachers?

But it's a myth that people are more creative when they know less. Creativity in any field is based on knowing a lot about that field. You can't create in a vacuum; you have to create in a subject, using knowledge in that subject. The most exceptional creators—from naturalist Charles Darwin to physicist Albert Einstein to painter Jackson Pollock—spent years learning what came before. But you can't just learn shallow knowledge, because creativity is grounded in *creative knowledge*: a set of understandings, cognitive structures, and habits of mind that are best learned as an integral part of teaching in every subject area.[1] When students first learn about the human body—for example, how the arm works—they focus on visible parts like the round bump of the elbow and the five fingers on each hand. With creative knowledge, students understand an explanatory model: how the design of the elbow joint restricts the range of motion; how the positioning of a weight, combined with the location where the tendon attaches to the bone, explains the amount of torque an arm can generate to lift the weight. They don't just memorize the formula that in a third-class lever, torque is a product of effort (the strength of the bicep) and the distance from the fulcrum (from the elbow to the point where the tendon attaches to the forearm) (Lehrer & Schauble, 2006).

Learning scientists have made great strides in understanding how creative knowledge can be taught and learned. In this chapter, I describe the creative knowledge we should be teaching, and how and why that knowledge supports creativity.

CREATIVE KNOWLEDGE AND SHALLOW KNOWLEDGE

Instructionism leads to shallow knowledge in a subject. And shallow knowledge does not support creativity. Fortunately, research now shows us the kind of knowledge that does: it's creative knowledge, and it's different from shallow knowledge in just about every way.

Creative Knowledge is Deep Knowledge

With creative knowledge, you understand the material you're learning, and you know *how* to think with it. With shallow knowledge, you memorize events that happened; with creative knowledge, you can explain why these events took place. Shallow knowledge includes a lot of facts that you've memorized; with creative knowledge, you understand where these facts came from and how we know that they're true.

> Education with inert ideas is not only useless, it is above all things harmful. Let the main ideas which are to be introduced be few and important, and let them be thrown into every combination possible.
>
> (A.N. Whitehead, 1929, pp. 1–2)

Shallow knowledge is a collection of facts about the world, such as the following:

- The correct spellings of words
- The locations of the letters on the standard QWERTY keyboard
- The multiplication tables
- The chemical structure of water (H_2O)

Personally, I think that students need to learn all of these things. I'm sure that you can add your own very long list. If teaching for creativity means that we have to stop teaching for subject-area knowledge, then creativity is going to lose out every time. It's a common criticism of progressive education that it's not rigorous enough, and that students don't learn important facts and skills.

My good news is that there's no conflict between teaching for creativity and teaching facts. Students don't become less creative when they memorize facts. And students don't become more creative when you stop teaching them facts. To be creative in a subject, you need to memorize a lot of shallow knowledge. Students need to learn vocabulary to be literate, and many creative writers use a larger vocabulary than the rest of us. Students need to memorize a lot to do math calculations, including the multiplication tables, or the procedures for how to add fractions. I use this kind of knowledge when I'm out in the garage, measuring parts for my craft projects.

Creative knowledge includes shallow knowledge—the same facts, skills, and procedures that are taught in instructionism. But unlike in instructionism, these pieces of knowledge aren't isolated chunks; they're linked together in rich conceptual networks. They form patterns that give them depth and meaning.

Creative Knowledge is Big Knowledge

From studies of scientific expertise, we know that scientific creativity is grounded in *bundles* of knowledge, not small pieces of shallow knowledge. Cognitive psychologists call the small pieces of shallow knowledge *chunks* (Gobet et al., 2001), and disconnected chunks of knowledge don't support creativity. Chunks are the elemental "atoms" of knowledge, the smallest thing that can be learned. In shallow knowledge, each chunk is very small. In science, such chunks include naming the kinds of clouds or the three kinds of rocks, or knowing how to spell *cirrus* (clouds) and *metamorphic* (rocks).

In instructionism, students learn small pieces of knowledge, one by one, one after another. In guided improvisation, students learn the same chunks of shallow knowledge that they would learn from instructionism, but they learn those chunks bundled together in a broader understanding of the subject. Creative knowledge brings together chunks of shallow knowledge in bundles that form complex wholes. Instructionism teaches students to memorize the names of each of the 50 states in the United States—their shapes, the names of their capitals, and what year they joined the union. But with creative knowledge, students will understand how to think about the social and political dynamics that resulted in the creation of that state, and why the state has the shape it does. I still remember winning a prize in elementary school, when I memorized the 50 state capitals. But I didn't understand much about the history of the states until a few years ago, when I started watching the wonderful TV show *How the States Got Their Shapes*.

Creative knowledge includes a lot of shallow knowledge. But those chunks of knowledge are connected into rich conceptual structures where students can see why they're learning it, and how it makes sense in a deeper conceptual structure.

Creative Knowledge Is Connected Knowledge

With instructionism, chunks of shallow knowledge are mentally disconnected and isolated from each other (Pellegrino & Hilton, 2012). Students don't learn how knowledge is related in complex systems. They don't learn the big picture.

A few years ago, I spent a couple of weeks helping Jerry, a middle school student, learn math. First, we learned how to add, subtract, and multiply fractions, like 3/8 or 18/72. Next, we learned how to do the same operations with decimals, like .25. Finally, we learned how to do these operations with percentages, such as 40% or 75%. At the end of each of the three units, Jerry scored a perfect 30 out of 30 on his worksheet.

Of course, fractions, decimals, and percentages are just different ways to represent the same number: ½ equals .50 equals 50 percent. I thought that Jerry knew that, too. But as we talked after finishing all three units, I was surprised to discover that Jerry didn't realize that these three math units were related. He thought he had learned three unrelated math procedures.

If we don't teach the underlying concepts that connect these three units, then why should we expect a student to learn those concepts? After all, Jerry learned what he was told, and he got a perfect score on each of the homework assignments. If you teach math procedures as disconnected and shallow chunks of knowledge, and you assess only for shallow knowledge, then students are unlikely to learn the underlying concepts that capture the connections.

Creative Knowledge Is Flexible

Creative knowledge is flexible and adaptable. Students learn that each subject's knowledge is dynamic and ever-changing. Students understand that new knowledge emerges from a creative process, the same creative process that they're learning themselves. Psychologists refer to this as *adaptive expertise*: knowledge that can be adapted for each novel situation (e.g., Schwartz, Bransford, & Sears, 2006).

When students learn only shallow knowledge, they learn it as something fixed and taken-for-granted, something that was discovered by really smart people in the past. Students don't realize that the knowledge they're learning originated from a creative process—the discoveries of scientists, the inventions of engineers, the insightful analyses of historians, the proofs and formulas of mathematicians. They don't learn that all knowledge is created, and they could never imagine that they could create knowledge, too.

Shallow knowledge is permanent and fixed. It's *brittle*—you can't alter a chunk of small knowledge without breaking it and making it useless. Buildings made of brittle material are more likely to collapse in an earthquake; if they're instead made with flexible material, they'll sway back and forth, but they won't break and fall over. This is why shallow knowledge doesn't *transfer* to new settings and problems. Students can apply shallow knowledge only to situations that are essentially identical to the context of learning. In contrast, creative knowledge can be modified and adapted to each new problem. It's similar to the contrast between skill and understanding. For example, when a person first learns to play basketball, they focus on dribbling the ball, shooting the basket, and passing to teammates. Knowing these things doesn't help you play football or hockey any better. But with experience, athletes begin to develop deeper understandings that transfer to other team sports. For example, they understand a core defensive strategy: Always close up available space for the offense (example from Wiggins & McTighe, 2005). This is when you move beyond simple technique, and you start to be a creative player, like Yuri Lavrinenko, the NCAA men's soccer championship tournament's outstanding offensive player in 1999:

> When I got the ball in midfield and I started dribbling, I was looking to pass right away. But my teammates opened up space, and I continued running. When I played the ball to Alexei, 2 players went to him and opened up more space for me. (Quoted in the *New York Times*, Dec. 13, 1999, p. D2; citation in Wiggins & McTighe, 2005)

The big idea is "creating and constraining offensive space," and it applies to basketball, ice hockey, soccer, water polo, football, lacrosse, rugby, and field hockey: When you're on offense, try to get someone on your team open, using moves and fakes. When you're on defense, always make sure that offensive spaces are closed up. Whether defense or offense, this deeper understanding prepares you to respond to the other team creatively, even though it rarely looks exactly like the drills you did in practice. When you learn creative knowledge, you can understand and see patterns that connect the surface details of different situations.

Creative Knowledge Supports Thinking and Acting

Creative people know how to think with what they know. They know how to solve new problems they haven't seen before. They know what they don't know, and what questions to ask. When students have creative knowledge, they're able to think like experienced creators in the subject.

I've talked to scientists, engineers, and artists, and they all say that being creative means *knowing how to think with* disciplinary knowledge. "How to think" is active and dynamic. It's filled with potential to drive forward to the future. Shallow knowledge is inert, static. You can't *do* anything with it. It looks toward the past, not the future.

Creative thinking means going beyond the given information, bringing together existing ideas into new combinations, and approaching novel problems by applying basic underlying frameworks and concepts of deep understanding.

Creative Knowledge Prepares for New Learning

When students learn creative knowledge, it prepares them for continued learning. When they're learning related knowledge in the next class or unit, they're better able to learn and understand it. After students have been learning for creative knowledge for a few weeks, or a semester, each unit's learning outcome starts to drive forward, so that creative knowledge builds on itself. Because creative knowledge is deep and flexible, the conceptual connections to the next unit become clear.

In a 9th-grade math class at a highly successful public school, students were asked to invent their own ways to quantitatively measure the variability of different phenomena along a linear scale (Schwartz & Martin, 2004).[2] Instead of giving a lecture, the teacher asked the students to figure out how to solve the problem on their own. The teacher didn't guide them toward the correct solution; instead, she asked them to explain what they were doing, or asked them whether their invented procedures aligned with their own "common sense," or pushed them to develop more general solutions (p. 138). Different student groups came up with different solutions, and the different groups didn't always notice the same quantitative properties (p. 145).

In traditional instruction on measuring variability, the teacher and the textbook would have simply given them the formula for mean deviation and had them memorize it (see Figure 2.1). But in this creative classroom, before they were taught the formula, these students were asked to figure out one of the following two problems, Problem 1 or Problem 2, on their own.

Figure 2.1. The Formula for Mean Deviation

$$\frac{\Sigma \ |x - \bar{x}|}{n}$$

Table A1. Data for Track Stars Problem

Top High Jumps in 2000		Top Long Jumps in 2000	
Height	Number of Jumps	Length	Number of Jumps
6'6"	1	21'6"	1
6'8"	2	22'0"	2
6'10"	3	22'6"	2
7'0"	5	23'0"	9
7'2"	6	23'6"	9
7'4"	7	24'6"	4
7'6"	4	25'0"	1
7'8"	1	25'6"	1
8'0"		26'6"	

Source: Schwartz & Martin, 2004, p. 176.

Problem 1. Track Stars
Bill and Joe are both on the U.S. Track Team. They also both broke world records last year. Bill broke the world record for the high jump with a jump of 8 feet. Joe broke the world record for the long jump with a jump of 26 feet, 6 inches. Now Bill and Joe are having an argument. Each of them thinks that his record is the best one. You need to help them decide. Based on the data in Table A1, decide if 8 feet shattered the high jump record more than 26 feet, 6 inches shattered the long jump record. (Schwartz & Martin, 2004, p. 175)

Problem 2. Getting Good Grades
Students had to decide which chemistry class Julie should take if she wants to receive a good grade. They saw the grades given by two different teachers the previous year. This problem introduced new challenges. Not only did students have to decide whether Julie would prefer Mr. Carbon's high-risk, high-payoff grading scale, they also needed to handle nonquantitative data with unequal sample sizes.

Mr. Carbon: A+, A+, A-, C+, C+, C+, C, C, C-, C-, C-, C-, D+
Mrs. Oxygen: B+, B, B, B, B, B-, B-, B-, B-, C, C, C-, C-, C-, D+,
D+.
(Schwartz & Martin, 2004, p. 179)

After working on one of these problems, all of the students listened to a lecture on the standard formula to measure variability. Then a group of researchers checked to see whether the 9th-grade students were able to apply their knowledge to novel problems: They gave a test where the students had to work with *two* variables instead of just one, "Homerun Hitters" below. Solving these questions requires the concept of covariance in bivariate data, which the students hadn't been explicitly taught. Thirty-four percent of the 9th graders invented a way to measure covariance, which is a pretty complicated concept (pp. 158 and 161).

Problem 3. Homerun Hitters
People like to compare people from different times in history. For example, did Babe Ruth have more power for hitting home runs than Mark McGuire? It is not fair to just compare who hit the ball the farthest, because baseballs, bats, and stadiums are different. Mark McGuire may have hit the longest homerun, but this might be because people use bouncier baseballs these days.
     Two people were arguing whether Joe Smith or Mike Brown had more power. Joe Smith's longest homerun was 540 ft. That year, the mean homerun among all players was 420 ft long, and the average deviation was 70 ft. The average deviation indicates how close all the homeruns were to the average. Mike Brown's longest homerun was 590 ft. That year, the mean homerun was 450 ft, and the average deviation was 90 ft. Who do you think showed more power for his biggest homerun, Joe Smith or Mike Brown? Use math to help back up your opinion. (Schwartz & Martin, 2004, p. 184)

This same bivariate problem, which required a deep knowledge of variance, was given to students at a top university, after they'd finished a course in statistics. And guess what: Only 12% of the college students created a workable solution! That shows that bivariation and covariance are complicated concepts, but it's still surprising that almost three times as many 9th graders solved it. The researchers suggested that the college students did worse because their statistics classes were taught using instructionism (Schwartz & Martin, 2004, pp. 158, 162). In contrast, the 9th graders learned creative knowledge. They explored and invented their own way of solving problems, with the teacher giving guidance but not giving right or wrong answers, and so the 9th graders had learned a more creative deep knowledge. They understood underlying concepts of linear distributions, like "central tendency" and "variability," and their understanding was so powerful that they were better prepared than top college students to create beyond what they'd learned.

Creative Knowledge Supports Interdisciplinarity

Creative knowledge prepares you to connect knowledge in one subject to related knowledge in other subjects. Studies of scientific innovation have found that many of the most creative ideas come from making interdisciplinary connections between bodies of knowledge. Creativity researchers call these new ideas *remote associations*, and research has shown that remote associations are more creative than new ideas that combine similar knowledge.

> At Olin College of Engineering half the students create interdisciplinary majors like Design for Sustainable Development and Mathematical Biology. The college has also led the way in creating new interdisciplinary concentrations, like bioengineering.
>
> (Wagner, 2012b).

This is why some of the most successful creative classrooms teach interdisciplinary knowledge, using activities in which students have to creatively combine knowledge in different subjects. When you work on problems that require multiple bodies of knowledge to solve, you have to construct deep knowledge in each of those subjects. Some of the most effective lesson plan designs are across subjects.

With creative knowledge, your deeper understanding prepares you to see the relationships between (for example) the molecular structure you've learned in chemistry and the structure of atoms in an electric current. It helps you understand how historical and cultural context (learned in social studies) influences literary style (in language arts class).

Interdisciplinary insights are much more likely when you have creative knowledge in multiple fields. Because creative knowledge in each field is adaptable, it can be modified or "stretched" so that you can connect it to different knowledge in a different field. When an entire school teaches creative knowledge in every class and every subject, a student's creative potential multiplies. They're prepared to be creative in each subject, but they're also prepared to be creative by connecting subjects. The connections between creative knowledge result in synergy, and the whole is greater than the sum of the parts.

MOVING BEYOND THE COVERAGE TRAP

In instructionist schools, the goal is to cover as much subject-area knowledge as possible, in the shortest amount of time. I call this the *coverage*

PICKING TOMATOES

A team of engineers was trying to design a mechanical tomato picker that didn't bruise the tomatoes when collecting them. They came up with some really creative solutions, but none worked. Eventually, a few botanists were brought in. Together, they reframed the problem: Why not try to breed a new kind of tomato, one with a skin that's less likely to get bruised? With this new problem framing, the interdisciplinary team in fact did develop a new type of tomato with a thicker skin that doesn't bruise as easily.

(Adams, 2001, p. 24).

---

trap, and can sometimes be even more of a trap in the best schools, with the best students and the highest test scores. The reason it's a trap is because if students master a lot of shallow knowledge, and then they're tested for how much shallow knowledge they've learned, it seems like instructionism is working fine. This can make it difficult to argue for a transformation to teaching for creative knowledge, with its focus on depth rather than breadth. Instructionism can seem effective at covering lots of shallow knowledge quickly, as long as students are tested immediately after the unit and semester end, before they inevitably forget most of the shallow knowledge they were taught. If a school's students are doing well on these tests, then it's often taken as evidence that it's a good school. Parents and administrators become overconfident: If we're doing so well, then nothing needs to dramatically change. Of course, even top schools will try to keep getting better—but improvement is thought of as either doing instructionism better or as increasing the scope of coverage.

In the 1960s, medical educators studied how much their first-year medical students remembered, of the thousands of new terms that they'd memorized in their first-year gross anatomy class. They were tested and retested over time. The results showed the failures of the coverage trap: they very quickly forgot almost everything they'd "learned." When this data was published, it made a big impact on medical education, and today anatomy is taught in a dramatically different way (Shulman, 1999, p. 13).

The most effective schools don't think about learning in terms of coverage. Instead, they emphasize creative knowledge, depth over breadth. Surprisingly, researchers have found that these students score just as well on today's tests of shallow knowledge, even though the class didn't "cover" as much material. How could that be? It's because students can use their deep knowledge to derive shallow knowledge from the underlying principles.

The Finnish miracle in education is a powerful example of what's possible when a school turns away from emphasizing coverage (Sahlberg, 2011). Finnish students score at the top of the international rankings on the Program for International Student Assessment (PISA), which is administered in

---

TEACH LESS, LEARN MORE

When Singapore's Ministry of Education transformed their school system to teach creativity and innovation, they called it the Teach Less, Learn More initiative. To foster creativity, they realized that they have to reduce the focus on coverage, and instead focus on core knowledge, understanding, and critical thinking.

(Singapore Ministry of Education, 2005, 2015;
Tan, Tan, & Chua, 2008; Trilling & Fadel, 2009).

---

over 70 countries (OECD, 2008); U.S. students score right in the middle of the pack. PISA isn't just a multiple-choice test of memorization; it assesses deep, creative knowledge (Ripley, 2013). Finnish classes cover less material; students have fewer hours of instruction, and of homework, than almost every other country. They don't even start school until they're 7 years old. Finnish teachers teach less too: about 600 hours annually, whereas U.S. teachers teach 1,080 hours. That's the difference between four courses a day and six courses a day. The Finnish teachers aren't just going home early; they're planning the next day, and developing their own lessons, curriculum, and assessments.

According to the Trends in International Mathematics and Science Study (TIMSS), which compares student achievement in math and science in 50 countries every 4 years, U.S. science and math curricula cover a lot more chunks of shallow knowledge than other countries (Stigler, Gonzales, Kawanaka, Knoll, & Serrano, 1999). In other countries, educators sometimes say that curricula in the United States are "a mile wide and an inch deep," in contrast to their own schools, which focus on deep understanding and creative knowledge (Vogel, 1996). In 2015 the American Association for the Advancement of Science (AAAS) argued that this shallow approach doesn't work; this group of leading scientists was critical of goals of "coverage" and "overviews of the discipline" because it results in a pedagogy that makes it difficult, even impossible, for students to learn connections across concepts and to link together facts and ideas into deeper conceptual networks (Cooper et al., 2015, p. 281; also see President's Council of Advisors on Science and Technology [PCAST], 2012).

The U.S. focus on coverage doesn't work for creative knowledge, and it's not that effective at teaching shallow knowledge, either. As I showed in Chapter 1, students have poor retention, depth of understanding, and very poor ability to apply what they've learned outside of school. Rather than strengthening students' abilities, instructionist teaching has made U.S. students weaker in achievement compared to other countries. Studies of the TIMSS data show that children in nations that focus on creative knowledge do substantially better on the mathematics assessment than do U.S. children

(Schmidt & McKnight, 1997). In Finnish schools, usually ranked in the top five or ten best in the world, each year's learning outcomes focus on a few big concepts, and they emphasize deep understanding for creative knowledge (Sahlberg, 2011). Adding more shallow knowledge to the curriculum doesn't help students learn any better.

LEARNING CREATIVITY AND STATE STANDARDS

The National Inventors Hall of Fame School in Akron, Ohio, is one of the top three schools in Akron, based on raw state test scores. Forty-two percent of its students live in poverty. The school succeeded in serving these students by redesigning their pedagogy to emphasize creative knowledge instead of shallow knowledge (Bronson & Merryman, 2010, p. 47).

In one example, a group of teachers worked to develop an open-ended project for 5th grade. They designed a challenge, aligned with Ohio's state curriculum requirements, that the students dealt with every day: How can we reduce noise in the library? The library was unusually noisy because its windows looked out onto a busy public space. It was noisy even with the windows closed. There was no obvious solution, so the students had to think outside the box.

The teachers designed a 4-week unit to work on the project, providing students with the time necessary to work through an iterative, unpredictable creative process. Because the project took 4 valuable weeks of school time, teachers designed a creative process where students mastered a wide range of Ohio state standards and, at the same time, engaged students in several creative habits of mind:

> *Awareness.* The students started by looking for relevant data, guided by the teachers through an inquiry process that led them to creative knowledge of a range of science concepts. As they explored, they learned a lot of subject-area knowledge. How does sound travel through materials? What materials reduce noise the most?
> *Divergent thinking.* The students then generated lots of potential solutions, in a creative thinking style known as *divergent thinking.* Would it work to hang drapes over the windows? What if there were large plants next to the windows? In an effective creative process it's important to generate crazy ideas that seem like they would never work, and the students came up with long lists of ideas, like: What about hanging big kites from the ceiling? Could we buy an immense aquarium filled with fish to replace the window?
> *Asking good questions.* Students were guided by teachers to think about ways to reformulate the problem. For example, instead of exploring ideas to reduce noise, isn't the real problem that students

get distracted? Maybe the library's function could be redefined, as a place where learning was loud and active, instead of silent and solitary. Maybe the noise wouldn't be a problem if you played a soundtrack of something relaxing, like a waterfall.

Experimentation. The teachers were then prepared to guide the students to the next step in the creative process: They created quick models and prototypes, with inexpensive materials like corrugated cardboard boxes, paper straws, and toothpicks.

At the end of this process, each team had translated their creative ideas into reality, and they presented their proposed solution to their teachers and parents. The final solutions weren't wild and crazy; the teachers had guided the students toward relevant content knowledge, and their proposals actually had potential. The teams had identified challenges and limitations that would need to be explored moving forward. For example, they realized that for the plant or the fish tank ideas to work, a big challenge was that someone would have to care for them during the summer, and whenever the janitor was on vacation.

As the teachers guided the students through the creative process, the students learned creative knowledge in science: important elements of the Ohio's state standards for 5th-grade curriculum. Their creative knowledge learning outcomes included understanding sound waves and material composition (science); estimating the costs of materials using equations like per-unit calculations and percentages (math); and writing a convincing description of their proposed solution (language arts).

CREATIVE HABITS OF MIND

The National Inventors Hall of Fame school shows how guided improvisation can lead students through the creative process, at the same time as they learn subject-area knowledge. And by engaging in the creative process, students are guided through several domain-general habits of mind that increase creativity in every subject. These habits of mind help students better engage in the improvisational and exploratory process that builds on creative knowledge to drive forward to successful creativity.

Guided Improvisation

Studies of creativity have shown that ideas, inventions, and creative problem solving result from a process that's improvisational and unpredictable: a zig-zagging path. Creativity doesn't emerge predictably from a linear path from insight to execution. Instead, successful creators *iterate* through a nonlinear process where they revisit the same moment in the process multiple times, each time with fresh eyes. Creators encounter dead ends and they make mistakes; they start again and they always move forward (Sawyer, 2013).

That's why the Noisy Library project asked students to start out with wild and crazy ideas: The creative path isn't linear. The teachers didn't ask students to come up with a 4-week plan at the beginning of the unit, because creativity rarely happens when you start out planning a complete path from beginning to end. The teachers guided students through an improvisational process with unexpected developments. The students noticed new things in the environment that they didn't know were important when they started. Many student groups realized that they'd started out approaching the problem all wrong, and they changed their focus to try out a different path. In creative learning, students encounter dead ends, and sometimes develop incorrect answers and concepts. But when they eventually learn the correct solutions, they have a deeper understanding, and they're prepared to create with that knowledge.

Question Finding

The most surprising creative ideas happen when you start working without knowing exactly how to think about your problem. When students get stuck solving a problem, the most common reason is that they're asking the wrong question. In a 1985 study, middle school students who used an iterative, exploratory process were more likely to reformulate their problem and come up with new questions. This led them to create more original solutions to problems, when compared to students who made up their minds early on, and stuck with their chosen path until they were done (Moore, 1985).[3] Teachers can help students along by asking them to explain their question, and by asking them whether or not their solution matches "common sense" (Schwartz & Martin, 2004). The most successful creativity comes from discovering a new problem, asking a new question, or formulating the situation differently. It's better if teachers don't spell out the project's question for the students; when you instead guide them through the improvisational creative process, the students come up with their own questions while engaging in the work.

Mindful Awareness

Creative people notice a lot that's going on around them. For example, in the Noisy Library project, when teachers guided students to look away from the window, one student looked up at the ceiling and got the idea to hang kites. Even when they're focused on a particular task, creative people frequently look up and around, and scan the horizon. They notice interesting things, even things that are not obviously related to their creative challenge.

When you notice that students are too focused on getting the right answer and they're trying to finish the problem as quickly as possible, consider asking them to sit back, take a breath, and look around for a minute or two.

Playfulness

Creative people are always trying new things. They experiment in ways that aren't obviously going to drive them forward down a linear path. They explore the problem space, they scan the environment, and they come up with small ideas along the way. When students start going down a path that that they aren't sure leads to the solution, they have to continuously engage with content-area knowledge to determine what they need to know to keep going, or whether they should turn back and try a different way forward. Once students have developed a list of quick and simple ideas, teachers can guide students to play with ways to combine these small ideas together to result in deeper, bigger, creative solutions that are based in creative knowledge.

Accepting Failure

In the creative process, you'll have many ideas that will turn out to be meaningless or irrelevant. Sometimes they turn out to be just plain wrong. Creative people know that sometimes they'll spend time going down a dead end. They don't get too depressed or frustrated, because they know this is a necessary part of a process of exploration and frequent idea generation. But because each failure is small—because they're not trying to solve the problem with one big solution that requires a large investment of time—they can recover and continue forward.

In fact, teachers can take advantage of a student's wrong answer and teach them more deeply using that wrong answer than if they'd gotten to the right answer immediately. Studies of *productive failure* show that students can learn creative knowledge more effectively from mistakes than from getting to the correct answer right away (Kapur, 2008). The key is to guide them in exploring why their answer was wrong and how it's different from the right answer. Students don't learn from failure if the teacher focuses only on the right answer and ignores the student's wrong answer (Wallis, 2017). This research shows that if failures are handled well, students learn deeper, creative knowledge (Sawyer, 2018a).

Time to Experiment and Iterate

The creative process takes time. You can't know when it's going to end because you don't know if you've posed the right question, you don't know if you have the information you need to solve it, and you don't know what a good solution might look like. The Noisy Library project gave students

4 weeks, so that they could experience an authentic creative process, one that's inefficient and slow. Because effective learning takes time, the best assignment designs actually *prevent* students from rushing through their homework (Brown et al., 2014). That's why the teachers didn't ask students to think of a good idea at the beginning and develop a linear plan toward a solution, one that would lead most efficiently and quickly to a good answer. The Noisy Library project guided students to think deeply, rather than trying solve the problem using shallow knowledge of a fixed procedure that they'd memorized from instructionism.

CREATIVE KNOWLEDGE IN MATH, SCIENCE, AND HISTORY

In guided improvisation students engage in hands-on activities that they develop, and they apply these creative habits of mind to the subject-area knowledge that they're learning. If you start out by teaching students shallow knowledge, and then later teach them these habits, it's too late: The creative mindsets work best when they build on creative knowledge. Students need to learn subject-area knowledge and creative habits of mind through the same activities. That's why in creative schools every subject is taught differently, leading students toward creative knowledge in each subject. Students learn the required content knowledge as creative knowledge, not shallow knowledge.

Creative Knowledge in Math

Bob Knight, a middle school teacher at Colter Bay Junior High School, teaches algebra by guiding students through an improvisational creative process. In his classrooms students can't solve problems with a rote application of memorized formulas (Yinger, 1987, pp. 40–43). Instead, he gives them complex problems where they have to spend some time learning how to think about them. In fact, this is at the core of the Common Core State Standards in math, which emphasize learning to think mathematically, rather than simply learning formulas as shallow, memorized knowledge. When researcher Robert Yinger asked Mr. Knight why he taught using guided improvisation, he said it was the best way to teach the following aspects of mathematical thinking. It's fascinating that these are the same creative habits of mind described earlier in this chapter:

- Understanding the fundamentals
- Looking for different approaches to problems
- Knowing what approach to take when setting up a problem
- Applying concepts and making connections between them
- Making connections between concepts and processes learned in other units in the course

Mathematical creativity doesn't result from applying the formulas that are memorized in instructionist classrooms; it requires creative knowledge of math. Paul Halmos, one of the most influential mathematicians of the 20th century, wrote the following in his essay "Mathematics as a Creative Art":

> Mathematics is a creative art because mathematicians create beautiful new concepts; it is a creative art because mathematicians live, act, and think like artists; and it is a creative art because mathematicians regard it so. (Halmos, 1968, p. 389)

Creativity in math requires improvisation: spontaneous, cooperative action. Creative knowledge in math supports reasoning and argumentation (Knudsen & Shechtman, 2017, pp. 177–178). It prepares learners to improvise using math knowledge, and to construct their own knowledge.

Creative Knowledge in Science

In 2009 the leading U.S. scientists got together to figure out why students weren't learning science very well in school.[4] Of course, the students were taking science classes, and the best students got near-perfect scores on standardized tests. But these were instructionist classrooms, and these were tests of shallow knowledge. The scientists quickly realized what the problem was: Shallow knowledge doesn't help students understand science. If you learn by memorizing shallow knowledge, you don't learn that science is a creative process through time, a process that's based on creative knowledge, a process that is within anyone's potential. When all that you learn is shallow knowledge of science, you think that scientific knowledge comes from somewhere else, that it's true and unchanging. You think all that scientists do is observe the world and then write down what they see. You don't learn how to think like a scientist, or how scientific inquiry works, or how a scientist could ever be creative.

Creative knowledge in science is big, deep, and connected. The Next Generation Science Standards (NGSS) emphasize creative knowledge (e.g., National Research Council, 2012; NGSS Lead States, 2013). They argue that the most important learning outcomes of science education should be these seven *crosscutting concepts* (National Research Council, 2012, pp. 83–102):

1. Patterns
2. Cause and effect
3. Scale, proportion, and quantity
4. Systems and system models
5. Energy and matter in systems
6. Structure and function
7. Stability and change in systems

THE SUN IS A STAR: SHALLOW OR DEEP KNOWLEDGE?

The NGSS gives this example of a deep knowledge learning outcome, from 5th grade: "The sun is a star that appears larger and brighter than other stars because it is closer" (NGSS, 2013, p. 49). There are two shallow chunks of fact in this core idea:

- The sun is a star
- The sun is closer than other stars

A student can memorize these two facts. But when the student looks up at the sky, he might still think that the sun is a lot bigger than all of the stars. He can't transfer shallow knowledge to understand and explain real-world observations.

But in deep knowledge, these two facts are embedded in a network of concepts that allows students to understand their original misconception: The sun looks a lot larger and brighter than all of the stars in the sky, but it looks like it's bigger only because it's closer. Without deep knowledge, students can memorize the facts and do well on tests, but their misconceptions are never challenged.

These seven concepts are deep, connected, and adaptable. This kind of creative knowledge supports a range of creative scientific activities, including the following:

- Gathering and generating lots of data related to the problem (supported by divergent thinking)
- Interpreting and analyzing data (associated with combinatorial thinking)
- Forming concepts based on these data (based on imaginative thinking)
- Applying of general principles to specific cases (dependent on adaptive expertise)

Paul Wyatt, chemistry professor at the University of Bristol in the United Kingdom, told me that understanding in chemistry requires creative knowledge (personal communication, 2018). Year after year, the top students in the United Kingdom—the ones with the highest marks on the challenging A-level college entrance exams—enter his classes with confidence in their scientific knowledge. But Wyatt says that he can't trust the A-level exam scores because they test only shallow knowledge. The tests don't reveal that the students haven't learned *how* to think creatively with that knowledge. After years of teaching these students, he knows that it's because they've been in instructionist schools that teach only shallow knowledge. Because his students have learned only shallow knowledge, they can't solve

---

EXAMPLE: WHAT'S INSIDE THE EARTH?

The legendary educator Professor John Dewey frequently told this story in the 1930s, to support his claim that students have learned only shallow knowledge: While visiting a high school science class, he asked the students, "What would you find if you dug a hole in the earth?" The classroom was silent. None of the students attempted an answer, so Dewey repeated the question; still, silence. After this second time, the teacher politely turned and whispered to Dewey, "You're asking the wrong question." She then turned back to the class and asked, "What is the state at the center of the earth?" The students replied, in unison, "Igneous fusion." (Bloom, Engelhart, Furst, Hill, & Krathwohl, 1956, p. 29)

These students had learned such extremely shallow knowledge that they could only use it when they were asked exactly the same question, word for word, that they were taught. This story also shows that back in the 1930s, even teachers thought that shallow knowledge was the purpose of science education. Today, we know better!

---

authentic chemistry problems. And even when they're stumped, they're still confident that they have the necessary knowledge to solve it; they just think that they haven't applied it effectively. They think the problem is just like all of the other shallow-knowledge problems they've been taught—and that it requires just a bit more effort. But as they try harder and harder, they get more and more frustrated, because you can't solve creative problems with shallow knowledge.

Wyatt's experience is echoed by many studies of what high school students know. A 1994 study found that when high school graduates start college, they can solve well-structured problems that are just like the ones they worked on in school (King & Kitchener, 1994). But when they're given an open-ended problem, one that's ambiguous and doesn't have an obvious answer or a clear solution path, they're confused. Their only option is to use shallow knowledge that they've memorized, and they try to solve these problems as if they're well-structured.

Wyatt thinks that their shallow knowledge actually blocks their ability to be creative in chemistry. He has to *un-teach* them. It takes some work because the students are understandably resistant to leaving behind strategies that have caused them to be successful in their instructionist high school. Professor Karen Spear sees the same thing in her college courses. Her students have done well in big lecture classes using instructionism, and they've become very good at transcribing, memorizing, and regurgitating their lectures. But then they're lost when they get to the advanced courses, where they're expected to ask

> Thinking historically is counterintuitive. History requires understanding concepts that differ from everyday conceptions and explanations.
>
> (Carretero & Lee, 2014, p. 587)

original questions, or find novel solutions, or examine their own preconceptions. According to their professors, the students actively resist attempts "to get them to go beyond the information that we give them" (Spear, 1984, p. 7).

Creative Knowledge in History

Most students experience history as a series of unrelated names, dates, and places. They rarely realize that the professional study of history requires a lot of creative knowledge. Of course, historians need to know a long list of small chunks of knowledge: what events happened and on what dates; names of important people, how they became important, and what they did; locations on the map and how they're related; and many other chunks of shallow knowledge. But historical thinking requires you to understand a broad range of big, connected, and adaptable concepts that apply to many historical periods. For example, to understand thousands of years of European history, students need to learn the definitions of concepts like peasants, generals, laws, and priests.

Creative knowledge in history builds on these generalizable concepts, and brings them together in a number of core overarching concepts that organize together large numbers of chunks of shallow knowledge:

- *Change over time.* What causes change and what forms does it take? How does each historical event contribute to broader patterns of change?
- *Significance.* Which events have the most historical impact, and why? Why are we taught some events, but not others?
- *Conflicting individual accounts.* How does a person's location in society change how they perceive the same event? How should we evaluate each account's validity? How can we explain and reconcile differing accounts?
- *Historical evidence.* What kinds of documents, artifacts, and other records would be necessary to support a particular historical account? What documents did we not find that we should have found if a particular account is true? What should we look for to help us understand historical patterns and events, and where might it be?

Compare these core concepts to the NGSS science learning outcomes I described earlier, the seven crosscutting concepts. Creative knowledge in history, in science, and in math share the essential qualities that I introduced at the beginning of this chapter: connected, deep, big, flexible, and adaptable.

Historical understanding—just like the scientific understanding I described in the previous section—is a perfect example of why brittle knowledge doesn't support creativity. Shallow historical knowledge—the kind that's learned from instructionism—is a succession of memorized names, events, and dates. Students who are taught this way come to believe that in history, the general tendency is for things to stay the same. They don't realize how often things change over time. When they're asked to explain a dramatic historical change and what causal factors contributed to it, they have a lot of trouble. They usually respond by regurgitating the shallow facts they've learned. For example, they'll say that the change was caused by a particular person, on a particular date. For example, consider the question, "Why did slavery end in the United States?" Most students will say that Abraham Lincoln ended slavery when he issued the Emancipation Proclamation. Lincoln played an important role, but his actions can only be understood in the context of complex social, economic, and cultural forces. A few students might remember that Lincoln issued the proclamation on January 1st, 1863. But very few will be able to explain the military and political variables that Lincoln considered before deciding on this particular date. Students who learn only shallow knowledge don't learn to think in terms of larger cultural, societal, and material forces that play significant roles in historical change.

When students are taught history with instructionism, they don't learn how the various elements of history are connected. Students don't know how to develop explanations that incorporate politics, economics, and culture. In 2000, researchers asked a group of U.S. college students to explain why the Soviet Union broke up in 1991 (Voss & Carretero, 1998). None of the explanations mentioned interactions among factors such as economic problems, nationalism, or international context. These college students had learned only shallow knowledge. Without creative knowledge, they weren't prepared to develop deep and meaningful explanations. They didn't know what questions to ask, what information to gather, or how to proceed through a wandering, open-ended problem.

Without a deeper understanding of how to think historically, it's very hard to explain why two different people might interpret the same facts differently. Competing interpretations are particularly common between adversaries—like the United States and the USSR during the Cold War. After the Soviet Union broke up in 1991, Professor Jim Wertsch spent some time in Moscow, interviewing Russian high school students about World War II (Wertsch, 2002). One of his questions was: What role did the United States play in ending the war? American students say that we invaded France to open a second front against Germany to help Russia, and that our role was critical in defeating Germany. Russian students told Dr. Wertsch a very different story: They said that the United States waited until 1944 to invade Germany, even though it would have helped Russia a lot more if they'd invaded 1 or 2 years earlier. In their view, the United States waited until Russia had done all of the hard fighting. They say that the reason the United States waited is because their weapons manufacturers were making a lot of money selling weapons to Russia and other allies, and they would make more money if the war lasted longer. They only invaded because they were concerned that Russia would win by itself and dominate postwar Europe. Keep in mind, these interviews took place *after* Russia had abandoned Communism, and after the Cold War had mostly ended!

The stories of the Russian students included many of the same facts and dates that the American students learned. On a test of shallow knowledge, the Russians and the Americans would probably do equally well on the exact same test. But the shallow knowledge that they learned in school hadn't prepared them to evaluate different accounts and engage in argumentation. And after all, isn't this what we want all of our graduates to be able to do?

Our media's recent attention to "fake news" isn't the whole story of our political debates today. Even when different groups agree on the facts, they often construct different big-picture narratives, with dramatically different explanations and understandings. They disagree about which facts are most important, and on how the facts link together in a bigger, more complex conceptual structure. Engaging with different narratives requires creative knowledge. We need our students to learn to do a lot more than look up facts on the Internet.

TEACHING FOR CREATIVITY IN EVERY SUBJECT

Creativity tends to be specific to a domain—a discipline, subject, or field. That's why educating for creativity is more effective when it's integrated into every school subject, compared to teaching creativity as a general set of skills. When creativity training programs use activities and materials that focus on a specific subject, creativity in that subject is enhanced more than it is when students get domain-general creativity training (Sawyer, 2012, pp. 58–60). For example, in a 1996 study, psychologist John Baer found that training enhanced creativity, but only in the domain used in the training (Baer, 1996). Baer asked subjects ranging in age from 7 to 40 to create stories, poems, collages, and math word problems. He found that training on any one of those four areas increased the creativity of work in that area, but not in the other three areas.

Creativity can be extremely domain-specific. One study with middle school students found that after they were taught how to write more creative poems, the creativity of their poems increased. No surprise there! But this didn't enhance their creative writing ability in a general way; their short stories weren't any more creative than before. Another study found that people who wrote more creative short stories used different thinking styles than people who wrote creative nonfiction (Kaufman, 2002).

This is why it's misleading to say that children are more creative than adults. Creativity is domain-specific, and it's based in creative knowledge of the domain. This is also why it's misleading to say that schools block

Figure 2.2. Bloom's Pyramid

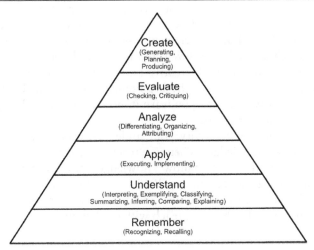

creativity, or that schools reduce a child's natural creativity. Yes, it's true that instructionist schools don't teach creative knowledge. But the problem isn't with school; the problem is with instructionism. In the next chapter, I describe guided improvisation, a pedagogy where students engage in activities that have a lot in common with children's playful explorations. The playfulness of childhood is, indeed, blocked by instructionism. But creative classrooms welcome a playful mindset in students because it has a lot in common with teaching and learning for creative knowledge.

In an instructionist school, sad to say, it almost doesn't matter how hard the teachers and the students work. The problem isn't the people, it's the pedagogy. Sometimes we assume that if students learn enough shallow knowledge—enough facts and procedures—that they'll gradually combine these small chunks of knowledge to form increasingly complex and deep knowledge. This is one of the main implications of Bloom's taxonomy (see Figure 2.2): Teaching should start at the lowest level of the pyramid because students need to learn shallow knowledge first (Anderson & Krathwohl, 2001; Bloom et al., 1956). After students have learned knowledge at one level, the assumption is that they're prepared to move up to the next level. The implication is that you can't learn to be creative until you've already learned everything else. When you think about learning this way, creative knowledge has to wait until the end of the semester. Only then are you ready to move to the top of the pyramid and learn to be creative with everything you've learned at the lower levels.

However, research has shown that all of these assumptions are false (Anderson & Krathwohl, 2001, pp. 287–294). Even David Krathwohl, one of the cocreators of Bloom's taxonomy, admitted that there was never any research showing that knowledge had to be learned from bottom to top. When Bloom and his colleagues wrote their report in 1956, they assumed that later research would eventually prove them right (Krathwohl, 1994, pp. 182, 191). But in fact, new research has shown that it's more effective to teach at the higher levels and the lower levels at the same time (Agarwal, 2019). To learn for creative knowledge, it's better to be taught creative knowledge right from the beginning. And even to learn shallow knowledge—the lower levels—you learn it more effectively when you learn it along with the higher levels.

When you teach for creativity, your students learn *both* creative knowledge and shallow knowledge. When you teach for creativity, students learn the facts and procedures of shallow knowledge even better than with instructionism (Pellegrino & Hilton, 2012). You don't have to choose between teaching for creativity and teaching for good scores on standardized tests. You can do both when you teach with guided improvisation.

NOTES

1. What I call "creative knowledge" is closely related to other terms and concepts used by learning scientists, including deep learning, powerful learning (Darling-Hammond et al., 2008), and three-dimensional learning (NRC, 2014). Much of the research that this chapter is based on was conducted by researchers using these terms and concepts.

2. Schwartz and Martin (2004) call this pedagogy "inventing to prepare for learning (IPL)" and describe it this way: "Rather than constructing a narrow path for success, as might be the case for materials that have a single correct answer, IPL is meant to provide a broad path that permits variation without spilling into chaos. . . . IPL materials are meant to permit flexibility in teaching styles." (pp. 145–146)

3. Moore's study was a replication of an earlier study with painting MFA students (Getzels & Csikszentmihalyi, 1976).

4. A few of the most influential reports are are are: *Next Generation Science Standards* (NGSS Lead States, 2013); *Successful K–12 STEM Education* (National Research Council, 2011); *A Framework for K–12 Science Education* (National Research Council, 2012); and *The Opportunity Equation* (Carnegie Corporation of New York, 2009).

CHAPTER 3

Guided Improvisation

The best teachers use improvisational teaching because their experience and their instincts tell them it's the most effective way to help students learn. Research shows that experienced teachers are more likely than novice teachers to use instructional strategies designed to guide improvisation. For example, their lesson plans are more open-ended, and they spend less time planning the details of each class session (Berliner & Tikunoff, 1976; Borko & Livingston, 1989).[1] Expert teachers have *adaptive expertise*: They've spent years designing and using lesson plans and classroom activities, and they've dealt with just about every crazy thing a student can do. But they use this pedagogical knowledge to extend, modify, and adjust their plans creatively, in an improvisational response to each unique situation (Bransford, Brown, & Cocking, 2000; Spiro, Feltovich, Jacobson, & Coulson, 1991).

Teaching for creativity isn't a matter of natural skill, or ability, or a particular type of personality. Teaching for creativity doesn't mean that you have to be an artist, a freethinker, or a bit eccentric. Every teacher can learn how to teach creative knowledge in their subject. In this chapter and the next, I describe how to use a set of classroom techniques that anyone can learn. I call this pedagogy *guided improvisation* because the students engage in open-ended activities, where they have freedom to improvise their own path through the material. But their actions aren't completely free and unconstrained. Student action is guided by structures, called *scaffolds*, that guide student knowledge construction toward curricular goals, while teaching them the knowledge that they need for creativity.

The research showing the effectiveness of guided improvisation and creative knowledge is overwhelming. It's on every page, and in every chapter, of the book I edited in 2014 called *The Cambridge Handbook of the Learning Sciences*.[2] It's the main theme of all of the recent scientific reports on how to teach effectively in math (Kilpatrick, Swafford, & Findell, 2001; NCTM, 2000–2004), in engineering (National Academy of Engineering, 2013), and in science (National Research Council, 1996).

I was surprised to learn that many teacher education programs don't spend much time showing teachers how to improvise with students. In fact, teaching method textbooks rarely mention flexibility, adaptability, or improvisational practice. One of my graduate students, Stacy DeZutter, analyzed

TEACHER MINDSETS ASSOCIATED WITH CREATIVE LEARNING

- Be open to unusual questions and ideas.
- Expect to be surprised.
- Build an environment of trust and safety.
- Support students in standing out against conformity.
- Reward curiosity and exploration.
- Build intrinsic motivation.
- Guide students in a reflective awareness of their own assumptions and fixations that often block new ways of thinking.
- Require students to generate lots of ideas, not only just one right answer.
- Give students time to think and time for incubation.
- Encourage risks and support mistakes and failure.
- Understand and develop ways to link creativity with content area knowledge. Students need to learn as much as possible about the subject that they're doing creative work in.[3]

14 teaching methods textbooks that are widely used in preservice teacher education programs, to see if any of them give teachers advice about how to adapt and respond flexibly in the classroom (DeZutter, 2011). Only one of the 14 books mentioned the need to adapt and improvise in class, and even that one had only a few sentences about it!

Instead of teaching the improvisational pedagogy used by expert teachers, all 14 of these textbooks emphasized the importance of advance planning. For example, one 597-page methods textbook (it shall remain nameless) devoted 100 pages to lesson planning. None of those 100 pages mentioned the need to develop flexible lesson plans that enable and guide student knowledge construction. In all 14 textbooks the discussions of classroom practice emphasized the need for teachers to develop a scripted and repeatable set of instructional strategies. The 597-page book devoted another 50 pages to instructional strategies, and these were all scripted and repeatable. The textbook had only one page that mentioned that teachers occasionally need to be flexible and responsive to students.

Teachers need to be able to plan lessons effectively, to be sure; but planning helps students much better if it's improvisationally adapted to each class, unit, and student. In Chapter 2 I showed that creative learning requires students to work through iterative, unpredictable, and improvisational activities. That's why each student's optimal path to creative knowledge might be different. Each student starts with a different set of knowledge, and each student might take a different path toward creative knowledge. That's why learning is most effective when the teacher improvisationally responds to each student's needs in each moment.

In Chapter 2 I showed that the creative process always takes place within constraints, and that learning for creativity is most effective when it's guided by parameters. Students learn creative knowledge more effectively when they're given freedom to improvise, but also when their improvisational learning process is guided with curricula, lesson plans, and instructional strategies.

Creativity training in a subject has been shown to enhance creativity, but only when the training is structured and directed (Scott, Leritz, & Mumford, 2004, pp. 380–381). For example, Karen Brennan's (2012) MIT dissertation found that creativity is reduced if you learn with too much structure. But she also found that *too little structure* reduced creativity. Without some structure, learners get lost. They aren't able to come up with ideas or follow through on ideas. But after a certain point, adding more structure starts to interfere with learning (Prieto, Villagrá-Sobrino, Jorrín-Abellán, Martínez-Monés, & Dimitriadis, 2011, p. 1225).

DeZutter's study of 14 methods textbooks shows that we have a long way to go to help teachers learn how to improvise in the classroom. But I'm encouraged that I'm starting to see more and more innovative teacher education programs that are helping teachers learn how to improvise. I think there's a lot of potential to expand these programs to all schools of education. Some successful professional development programs include the following:

- The legendary Second City Theatre in Chicago offers a series of workshops for teachers called "Improv for Creative Pedagogy" (www.secondcity.classes/chicago/improv-for-creative-pedagogy/). Teachers receive professional development credits from the Illinois State Board of Education.
- The Developing Teachers Fellowship Program (DTFP) at the Eastside Institute in New York City (eastsideinstitute.org/the-developing-teachers-fellowship-program/) had success teaching improvisational skills that educators could incorporate into their teaching as well as improv games that could be used as learning activities in the classroom (Lobman, 2011; also see Lobman & Lundquist, 2007). This program helped teachers become more collaborative with their students and better adapt their teaching for the unique needs of each class.

When preservice teachers practice improvisation in a safe space, guided by an experienced teacher, with other beginning teachers, they can become more comfortable with the ambiguity, uncertainty, and unpredictability of classroom improvisation. They learn that good teaching is a lot more than elaborate planning; it's an artful balance of structure and improvisation.

ART START

Art Start, founded in New York City by filmmaker Scott Rosenberg in 1991, is a nonprofit whose purpose is to help at-risk youth change their lives through the creative process. Rosenberg came up with this idea while teaching an art class at a last-chance school, an alternative high school for students who had dropped out or been expelled from other schools. Scott started out by giving projects where students engaged in unconstrained exploration and thought of wild and crazy ideas. Very soon he realized that this wasn't working. As he iterated and experimented, he added more and more structure. His approach is still improvisational, but he also says that it's rigorous and inquiry-based. After he added guidance to student creativity, Art Start became more effective at teaching creativity and higher-level thinking.

(Wagner, 2012a, pp. 142–143)

LEARNING TO IMPROVISE

I'm a jazz pianist, and after 40 years of playing, I know that jazz improvisation isn't a wild and free, unconstrained expression of inner demons or subconscious insights. Jazz improvisation balances structure with flexibility, and repetition with novelty. The best jazz players value the genres, songs, and players from the past. They're inspired by the structures of songs and the conventions of jazz. The most creative musicians have mastered the ability to perform within these structures and conventions. Jazz players don't consider these structures to be annoying limitations, to be rejected. They know from years of experience that these structures help them create more effectively.

It's a misconception that jazz musicians play from instinct and intuition, without conscious analysis or understanding. Jazz requires a great deal of training, practice, and expertise—it takes years just to play at a very basic level (Berliner, 1994). Even though I've been playing jazz piano for 4 decades, I'm still learning: I just learned a new way to use a diminished chord with a counterbass to transition between a II and a V chord on the way to the tonic at the end of a 16-bar chorus. (Don't worry, you're not supposed to understand that! That's my point—jazz performance involves a lot of specialized knowledge.) Jazz players have mastered a large repertoire of techniques like this, and they know there's always still more to learn. They have a deep knowledge of complex harmonic structures. They've mastered a large body of *standards*—pieces that have been played by jazz bands for almost a hundred years. In rehearsals, jazz groups often work out loosely composed ensemble parts, usually to begin or end a song. Many casual listeners will think that these sections are improvised; only the most knowledgeable jazz fans will know what's planned and what's improvised.

Today's players respect the past; they study how famous players have soloed on the same songs they're rehearsing. When the pianist in a quartet plays a melodic phrase from a piano solo from a well-known Count Basie recording, or plays an improvised riff in the style of McCoy Tyner, he's often anticipating that the other musicians will recognize it because experienced players have studied the same recordings. They don't frown at the lack of creativity of the pianist; instead, they're likely to smile in recognition of the clever placement of this small bit of melody from Basie, or the subtle homage to Tyner's genius.

In addition to these shared understandings, most jazz performers develop their own personal structures. In private rehearsals, they develop *licks*—melodic motifs that can be inserted into a solo for a wide range of different songs. Saxophonist Charlie Parker, one of the most creative players of all time, soloed using a personal repertoire of 100 motifs, each of them between 4 and 10 notes in length (Owens, 1974). Still, the choice of when to use one of these motifs, and how to weave these fragments into a new solo, is made on the spot.

In my first year of graduate school at the University of Chicago, I studied jazz improvisation by interviewing musicians and by watching live performances. But I didn't know the methods of musicological analysis, and I could only go so far with my studies of jazz. Fortunately, I was in Chicago, the world's top location for improv theater. I went to several performances, and I saw a lot of similarities with jazz. Improv groups create on stage as an ensemble as they exchange lines of dialogue, and take the performance in surprising new directions, as each performer responds to the others in ways that drive the scene forward. To learn more, I joined one group as the pianist, and I ended up staying there for almost two years. I videotaped live performances and interviewed actors. I transcribed their dialogues and analyzed the detailed, moment-to-moment conversational turns that were each improvised, but that built, magically, to an emergent collective creation. I learned that improv theater, like jazz, is more creative when it's guided by structures. All of the actors that I talked to emphasized the importance of structures, frameworks, and guidelines.

In guided improvisation, students are challenged with open-ended problems that they don't yet know how to solve. Each problem should be a bit ambiguous, so it's not immediately obvious what the solution should look like, or what path would be best to work toward a solution. The problem is designed to be complex enough that students can't solve it by applying a rigid procedure that they've memorized. Shallow knowledge doesn't help with an open-ended problem. Students have to use creative knowledge to solve it. To work through an open-ended problem, students need to engage in the creative habits of mind: They explore possibilities, formulate new questions, learn from and build on failure, reflectively examine their own understanding, and seek out additional information.

A good open-ended problem includes several parameters that limit and guide the student's creative solution process. Research shows that students learn best when their improvised explorations take place within carefully designed structures that are called *scaffolds*. Without guidance, a student might wander helplessly, become frustrated, and give up. Without guidance, a student could take a detour away from the subject matter entirely. Scaffolds guide student knowledge construction by directing them down an ex-

> "The hardest assignment would be to tell students 'Do a painting.' They'd get lost and frustrated. Students need structure to learn how to be creative."
>
> (An art professor at Washington University, quoted in Sawyer, 2018b, p. 156)

ploratory path that will lead them to construct the intended learning outcomes for the unit and the lesson plan (Davis & Miyake, 2004; Reiser & Tabak, 2014).

In guided improvisation, students learn their subject while they also learn how to identify good problems, how to ask good questions, how to gather relevant information, how to propose new solutions and hypotheses, and how to use domain-specific skills to express those ideas and make them a reality.

Guided improvisation is a great metaphor for good teaching because it emphasizes, first, that it's not planned in advance and, second, that the classroom is a collaborative improvisation. The students and the teacher collaborate in the improvisational creation of the unfolding classroom "performance." The teacher guides the classroom in a collaborative improvisation, one where she participates in collective knowledge construction, but participates in a way that artfully guides the students' learning improvisations.

Bob Knight, the middle school math teacher we first met in Chapter 2, is a master at guided improvisation. Every day, Mr. Knight taught six periods of 7th- and 8th-grade pre-algebra and algebra. Even though he taught pre-algebra and algebra—subjects that most people associate with the facts and procedures of shallow knowledge—he used an improvisational teaching style that emphasized deep concepts, connections across concepts, and creative application of knowledge to new problems. Mr. Knight's written plans had only a few penciled-in homework problems for the current week, and he rarely planned more than a week ahead. Each day, he made up on the spot the examples he used; he often didn't yet know the answers.

In addition to his flexible and open-ended lesson plans, Mr. Knight's improvisations were guided by a set of unwritten structures and techniques. For example, each unit followed the same pattern: *Individual lessons* → *Review lesson* → *First test* → *Test check* → *Second test* → *Test check*. And each lesson was structured in a three-part cycle of *Lesson presentation* →

Homework start → *Homework check.* But these structures weren't rigid scripts; Mr. Knight frequently improvised in ways that changed this structure. The "Homework check" was particularly improvisational, as Mr. Knight responded to each student question by creating a new problem on the fly, and working through that problem with the students. The mathematics educator Martin Simon calls this improvisational math pedagogy "the mathematical learning cycle," and his research supports Mr. Knight: This style of teaching leads to deeper mathematics understanding.

When guided improvisation is done well, observers often think that everything is planned and scripted in advance. For example, when outside observers visited Mr. Knight's classes, they often got the impression that he was working from a highly structured lesson plan (Yinger, 1987, p. 44). In my studies of improvisational theater, I saw something very similar: Audiences often think the performance is a lot less improvised than it really is. Especially when the performance comes off really well, and the improvisations result in the emergence of well-rounded characters and a coherent and believable plot, most people don't realize it was all created on the spot. They leave the theater thinking that "improvisation" means only a few embellishments on what is essentially scripted in advance (Sawyer, 2003). Likewise, when novice teachers observe an expert teacher's class, at first they think everything is carefully planned. It takes some time to develop the ability to see what's improvised and what's planned.

When teachers master guided improvisation, students learn creative knowledge. They gain a deeper conceptual understanding of the material and they retain it longer. When teachers are skilled at guided improvisation, students learn subject-area knowledge, they learn creative habits of mind, and they learn how to be creative with knowledge in that subject.

Guided improvisation raises test scores for all students, but it's particularly effective for increasing the performance and the engagement of lower-performing students. Sixth-grade teachers Leslie Stoltz and Mark Lantz at Chaparral Middle School in Walnut Valley Unified School District (CA) compared the standardized test scores of students in traditional classrooms, in 5th grade, with their scores a year later, after taking a guided-improvisation curriculum in 6th grade. (Davis, 2017, p. 164n1). All of the students got scores above those predicted from their 5th-grade scores, showing the effectiveness of guided improvisation. However, the gains for those students whose scores were above average didn't go up very much. But the learning gains were dramatic for students who scored below the average for their grade, and their scores were impressive in all three subjects that were tested. The benefits of guided improvisation continued all the way up to 8th grade, when these students scored higher on the standardized tests than students at the same school who had been enrolled in a traditional classroom.

COLLABORATION AND IMPROVISATION

If teachers are solo performers, up on stage improvising, that's just instructionism with a different performance style. The students aren't participating
and they aren't learning. The best teachers don't perform solo for a passive
audience; they guide all of the students in a group improvisation (cf. Gershon, 2006; Smith, 1979, p. 33).[4]

The following example, from an introductory 5th-grade math class
(Lampert, Rittenhouse, & Crumbaugh, 1996), is an example of students
and teacher jointly participating in an improvised conversation, and yet one
that is guided by the teacher's curricular goals for the lesson. The unit was
on functions, and the goal for this class was for students to learn the "divide
by two" function needed to solve this problem:

> Given four sets of number pairs, what is the rule—the function—to get
> from the first number to the second? The number pairs are 8-4, 4-2,
> 2-1, and 0-0.

Several small groups had trouble solving the problem. The teacher, Ms.
Lampert, had scaffolded the lesson using a sequence of activities, beginning with small-group discussion and then whole-class discussion. When
Ms. Lampert noticed the students' difficulty, she didn't simply give them the
answer; she guided them through the following improvisation:

1	Ellie	Um, well, there were a whole bunch of—a whole bunch of rules you could use, use, um, divided by two—And you could do, um, minus one-half.
2	Lampert	And eight minus a half is?
3	Ellie	Four
		(In response to this answer, audible gasps can be heard from the class, and several other students tried to enter the conversation.)
4	Lampert	You think that would be four. What does some-body else think? I, I started raising a question because a number of people have a different idea about that. So let's hear what your different ideas are and see if you can take Ellie's position into consideration and try to let her know what your position is. Enoyat?
5	Enoyat	Well, see, I agree with Ellie because you can have eight minus one half and that's the same as eight divided by two or eight minus four.

6	*Lampert*	Eight divided by two is four, eight minus four is four? Okay, so Enoyat thinks he can do all of those things to eight and get four. Okay? Charlotte?
7	Charlotte	Um, I think eight minus one half is seven and a half because—
8	*Lampert*	Why?
9	Charlotte	Um, one half's a fraction and it's a half of one whole and so when you subtract you aren't even subtracting one whole number so you can't get even a smaller number that's more than one whole. But I see what Ellie's doing, she's taking half the number she started with and getting the answer.
10	*Lampert*	So, you would say one half of eight? Is that what you mean? (Lampert and Charlotte alternate for three turns; then, Lampert checks in with Ellie, who again repeats her original answer; then Lampert calls on Shakroukh.)
11	Shakroukh	I would agree with Ellie if she had added something else to her explanation, if she had said one-half of the amount that you have to divide by two.
12	*Lampert*	Okay. You guys are on to something really important about fractions, which is that a fraction is a fraction of something. And we have to have some kind of agreement here if it's a fraction of eight or if it's a fraction of a whole.

The students propose different answers throughout the discussion. Lampert doesn't say which answers are right or wrong. Instead, she facilitates a collaborative improvisation among the students, with the goal of guiding them toward the social construction of their own knowledge. In fact, if you read closely, you'll see that she noticed an opportunity to guide students toward the construction of two concepts that weren't in the day's lesson plan: the use of variables in functions (in turn 11, Shakroukh proposes the variable "the amount that you have to divide by two"), and a fundamental insight about fractions—that it's always a fraction of something (an insight that Lampert collectively constructs with the students). The class hasn't learned about variables, and they haven't started the fractions unit yet, but thanks to Ms. Lampert's expertise in guided improvisation, the students will be prepared to make connections to underlying concepts when they begin the fractions unit.

In this example, creative knowledge emerges organically from student conversation. But studies of conversation and learning have had mixed findings. Some studies show that talk among students enhances learning, and others show that it doesn't. But there's new research that helps us understand these contradictory findings: Collaborative conversation sometimes seems to be ineffective in instructionist classrooms, but collaboration enhances deep learning when students are taught using guided improvisation. Collaboration doesn't always help students learn shallow knowledge, but it does help students learn better for deep knowledge (Kuhn, 2015; Pai, Sears, & Maeda, 2014; Phelps & Damon, 1989).

Researchers have extended constructivist theory to classroom collaboration and now conceive of learning as *coconstruction* because knowledge is learned in and by groups (Forman & Cazden, 1985; Hicks, 1995; Palincsar, 1998; Rogoff, 1998; Tudge & Rogoff, 1989; Verba, 1994; Wells & Chang-Wells, 1992). Children learn from collaborative discourse when there are multiple perspectives. Collaborative learning works best when the class activity is improvisational, with no predetermined outcome and no preset script. Student discussion must be allowed to take its own course, so that group learning can emerge from the interaction of the group (Bearison, Magzamen, & Filardo, 1986; Doise & Mugny, 1984; Perret-Clermont, 1980).

Guided improvisation is essential in class sessions where you have the students collaborate, because when student discussions are guided by the teacher, the research is convincing: Collaboration leads to creative knowledge (e.g., Azmitia, 1996). Collaboration is a skill that grows with practice, and through trial and error. Students learn better with collaboration if they engage in conversations regularly, rather than only in a rare class session every week or two (Kuhn, 2015).

IMPROV TECHNIQUES FOR TEACHERS

Teachers can learn to improvise by experimenting with the same rules that improv actors follow (Sawyer, 2003). Improv performances are more likely to be entertaining, dramatically coherent, and funny when everyone in the ensemble follows these guidelines. Aspiring improv actors are taught these techniques in their first improv acting class, and almost all actors that you'll see on stage have practiced and mastered these rules. Although they're called "rules," they're flexible, and they allow an unpredictable performance to emerge from improvisation. In other words, these stage performances are "guided improvisations," just like teaching for creative knowledge should be! That's why I believe that teachers can learn guided improvisation from the example of improv theater.

Yes, And

The most important rule of improvisation is "Yes, and." This rule emphasizes that in every line of dialogue, an actor should do two things: accept what was proposed by the previous actor, and build on it by adding something new.

Here's a good example of two experienced actors following the "Yes, and" rule.

> The beginning of a 5-minute scene. Lights up. Dave is at stage right, Ellen at stage left. Dave begins gesturing to his right, talking to himself.

1	Dave	All the little glass figurines in my menagerie, the store of my dreams. Hundreds of thousands everywhere! *[Turns around to admire his store.]*
2	Ellen	*[Slowly walks toward Dave.]*
3	Dave	*[Turns and notices Ellen.]* Yes, can I help you?
4	Ellen	*[Ellen is looking down like a child, with her fingers in her mouth.]* Um, I'm looking for uh, uh, a present?

Ellen's nonverbal offer in Turn 2—walking toward Dave—could be interpreted in many different ways. Early in a scene, actors are taught to make statements, or take actions, that have multiple possible meanings. Ellen's nonverbal entrance to Dave's store could lead to a variety of different scenes. In Turn 3, Dave accepts her walking movement, and proposes a new offer: she is a customer in his store. In Turn 4, Ellen accepts that she's his customer, and then builds on that idea by saying what she needs to buy.

Teachers who are expert improvisers instinctively follow the "Yes, and" rule. In the following example, Ms. Jones is guiding her class of 1st- and 2nd-grade students in an improvisational activity where they learn how bees communicate to each other as they search for nectar, collect it, and bring it back to the hive (Dahn, Enyedy, & Danish, 2018). The students were jumping around and dancing as they pretended to be bees. This bee dance activity is often found in elementary school classrooms, but this time it was dramatically different: the classroom had been outfitted with an *augmented reality* technology. Cameras in the room detected each student's movements, and then a computer program displayed each student, as an animated bee, on a projector screen. The projection of the computer simulation provided additional guidance to the students' improvisational dance—scientifically accurate and in real time. In the transcript below, you'll see Ms. Jones guiding the students' improvisational creation of a bee communication system. But this time, the students had created a communication system that didn't work. As the students watched the animation of the communication system they'd designed, they saw the bees wandering aimlessly, and they didn't find the flowers. In the transcript, Ms. Jones follows the "Yes, and" rule; she accepts the students' creation, even though it's incomplete, and then she builds on it by guiding the students' improvisation toward a correct understanding.

1	Ms. Jones	Adam got some. Dylan's going . . . *[Dylan walks back to hive]*
2	David	You have to fill it and then bring it back to the hive
3	Ms. Jones	What are you filling it with?
4	Many students	Nectar!
5	Ms. Jones	The honey?
6	Jesse	No
7	Ms. Jones	No honey?
8	Jesse	*[Leans in from yoga mat]* Oh, maybe that's the pollination you did! The . . .
9	Zed	Oh, pollen! *[Points to screen from yoga mat]*
10	Jade	Oh, I thought of something. *[Points to screen from yoga mat]* If you like go into there and fill up a lot of nectar
11	Jesse	*[Gestures toward the screen from mat]* When the little dots are coming out of you, that means You're pollinating
12	Ms. Jones	Oooh
13	Zed	Oh, I get it! *[Stands up to enter the space]*
14	Ms. Jones	Sit down, sit down. *[Gestures for Zed to sit down]* Use your words, use your words
15	Zed	*[Sits down]* I get this! I get this! So . . .

16	Ms. Jones	*[Crouches down toward Zed]* What do you get? What do you get?
17	Zed	*[Gestures toward the screen]* Um, the, when, if you, if hearts come out that means your, your, your pocket fills up with nectar and then you bring it from the . . . out and then and then a heart comes up and that means you fill the, the bees are filling the hive with nectar
18	Ms. Jones	Oooh there was some good observations that you just had right there.
19	Multiple speakers	*[Overlapping talk]*

No Denial

A companion to "Yes, and" is the rule "No denial." "Denial" is when an actor doesn't accept the previous line of dialogue. After you take your first few improv training classes, you know enough to not reject someone out of hand, but denial is still common—it's just implicit and subtle. In the next example, Dave uses various types of denial to reject Jack's creative contributions to the scene. You may have to read this closely; if you're not an improviser yourself, it can be hard to spot these subtle forms of denial.

These are the first eleven turns of a 5-minute scene. The audience has suggested "A Control Tower" as the location for the scene. When the lights come up, Dave is standing with his left hand on his ear, miming holding headphones. Facing the audience, he gives instructions to what is obviously an aircraft for about 30 seconds before Turn 1 below, when he puts down the headphones and begins to mix a cocktail. Then Jack enters at Turn 2.

1	Dave	Just a little liquid refreshments *[Dave mimes picking up a bottle and something else off a shelf]*
2	Jack	*[Jack walks on stage right]* Uh, excuse me? *[He is holding his pants up and slouching. Dave is shaking a cocktail]*
3	Dave	Yes, dude.
4	Jack	Uh, I believe I am the new trainee for the, uh, flight tower thing job, whatever you call it.

5   *Dave*   All right!
                Can you make daiquiris?
6   *Jack*   Oh . . . yeah,
                My last job was a bartender.
                [Dave picks up mixer and holds it in front of Jack for him to
                hold and shake it]
7   *Dave*   Okay good, 'cause I've been doin' it myself [and I] really
8   *Jack*   *[Jack takes the mixer from Dave]*
                [okay]
9   *Dave*   Yeah, and I really have to . . .
10   *Jack*   Ptchh
                [Jack takes mixer, starts to shake it, then makes sound effect
                Ptchh while swinging his right arm back over his head]
                Oh, I lost the top!
                [Turns to Dave]
                Sorry
                I, Is that, uh
                Eew
                [Jack points up and looks up, grimacing, as if to say "what a
                mess!"]
11   *Dave*   Oh, that's okay.
                We have another.
                [Returns arm to shelf and hands a second cocktail mixer to
                Jack]
                Here, hold this.

Did you spot the denials? I counted three, all by Dave. Here's what improv actors would say about Dave's performance.

In Turn 5, Dave uses a subtle form of denial known as *shelving*. He accepts Jack's proposal in Turn 4—that he is a trainee for a new job in the flight tower—but he immediately shifts the discussion to the topic of making drinks. Dave's turn doesn't explicitly reject Jack, but it's irrelevant both to being a trainee and to being in the flight tower. It's as if Jack hasn't done anything at all.

Turn 7 is another example of shelving. Dave accepts Jack's statement that he has experience as a bartender, saying "Okay good," but he doesn't build on Jack's statement. As in Turn 5, Dave continues in a different direction.

Dave's denial in Turn 11 is the most obvious. In Turn 10, Jack accidentally loses the top of the cocktail shaker, and he has spilled the drinks everywhere, even on the ceiling. Once again, Dave doesn't explicitly deny Jack's proposal, but he shelves it by saying "Oh, that's okay."

I've watched the video of this 5-minute scene many times, and Dave's denials continue for the whole scene. I can see Jack getting frustrated, even though the audience is laughing and seems to enjoy the performance. Dave has almost complete control over the direction of the scene, and the performance isn't collaborative at all.

Many teachers are committed to fostering a discussion culture in the classroom, and they work hard to accept and encourage their students' statements. But even for these teachers, it's easy to slip into these more subtle forms of denial. When a student offers a comment that isn't what you were expecting, and that could easily lead away you're your lesson plan, you might say "That's very good, Susan. Okay, now let's turn to our next problem . . ." Sometimes, you don't realize that you're doing it. Your students might not realize it, either, but subconsciously, they can see that their talk is being ignored. A more effective response would be to improvise a brief exchange that would guide Susan to see how her idea linked back to the prior discussion, and then, build on Susan's comment in a way that links it forward to the next problem in your lesson plan. This requires a deep understanding of the subject, and a confidence in your ability to adapt your lesson plan to improvise *with* the class, not *alone* while instructing the class.

To avoid these various subtle forms of denial, you can improvise together with the class. When you teach with guided improvisation, you'll establish a genuine and strong discussion culture in your classroom.

Don't Drive the Scene

In instructionist classrooms the teacher does most of the talking (Cazden, 2001). But if one improv actor did most of the talking, it wouldn't be an ensemble performance any longer. Actors embrace the collective creativity of improv, and they want each new scene to emerge unexpected from the improvised dialogue of all actors. Actors use the terms *playwriting* or *driving* when an actor takes over the scene leaving no room for the other performers to contribute to its direction. Driving usually comes along with denial; in the control tower scene above, Dave's frequent denials allow him to drive the scene.

Don't Endow

Endowing is to assign attributes, actions, or thoughts to another performer's character. Actors frown on this because it gives the speaker too much control, and it limits the creative options for the other performer. In the following example, the first four lines of Ann's Turn 1 are endowing.

The beginning of a scene with Ann and Donald. Donald has raised his hands in front of him, about two feet apart. Ann raises her hands, too, but about six inches apart:

1	*Ann*	I knew you when you were *this* big!
		[Shakes her hands for emphasis]
		I didn't know you when you were *that* big.
		[Pointing to the distance between Donald's hands]
		Your mom was in the maternity ward for *so long*.
		But listen, I knew you when you were *this* big.
		And you know what you said to me?
		The first thing you said to me?
2	*Donald*	What did I say to you?
3	*Ann*	Goo, goo.
		Oh, you were so cute, can you do that again?
		Just go "goo, goo."
4	*Donald*	Goo, goo?
		[Spoken tentatively, as if wondering if he is doing it right]

Turn 3, when Anne puts words in Donald's mouth and tells him what to say, is an extreme form of endowing. Improvisers frown on this so much that they call it *pimping*!

Don't Ask Questions

Actors are taught not to ask questions because it significantly narrows the next actor's range of possible responses. Even if the actor's question is open-ended—something like "What do you want to do next?"—it still limits the range of creative possibilities. The next actor now has to say something about what they'll do next, instead of other possibilities such as "I like the shoes you're wearing today," or "John was a real jerk yesterday," or any of hundreds of creative actions.

Students learn best from guided improvisations where teachers ask open-ended questions. But when teachers ask *known-answer* questions, the student has no room to improvise. Known-answer questions are common in instructionist classrooms: Teachers ask questions with known answers to assess student understanding, and then they give feedback on that answer. This instructional strategy is so common that it's known among education researchers as the *IRE sequence*, for "initiation-response-evaluation." The teacher starts the IRE sequence by calling on a student and asking a known-answer question with a single correct answer. The student can't improvise, but can only answer in the way that the teacher has "endowed."

IRE strategies are useful for teachers because it gives them control and it allows them to keep the class on track with their day's plan. IRE reduces the anxiety-inducing uncertainty of improvisation, while still engaging the students in a simple form of participation. If students know they might be called on, at least it keeps them from falling asleep! It also serves a behavior management function: It makes it obvious to all of the other students that they should stay quiet while the answering student talks. Moreover, it serves a curriculum planning function by keeping the teacher's preplanned lesson on track. And, finally, it can help a teacher by showing how much a student has learned. But it doesn't help students learn (Cazden, 2001).

There can be a fine line between open questions and known-answer questions. It's easy to slip into asking *pseudo-open* questions: questions that seem on the surface to be open-ended, but where you really are looking for a specific, single answer. For example, in one science class, the teacher asked "What can you tell me about a Bunsen burner, Alan?" It seems like it's open; it seems as if Alan can say anything about a Bunsen burner in response. But as the conversation continues, the teacher makes it clear that she was actually seeking a specific statement about the conditions for luminous and non-luminous flames (Barnes & Rosen, 1969, p. 24).

The best questions are those that ask students to think deeply and explain what they're thinking and doing. The legendary preschool teacher, Vivian Paley, gives an example of how to do this in her description of leading a discussion about the book *Tico and the Golden Wings* (Paley, 1981, pp. 25–26). In the middle of the discussion, Deanna claimed that Tico should have to give up his golden wings. Paley disagreed with Deanna, but instead of "denying" Deanna, Paley asked her to explain: "Why can't he decide for himself what kind of wings he wants?" This question requires Deanna to think more deeply. But it also requires Paley to give up some control over how the class improvisation unfolds.

Crossing the Fourth Wall

The *fourth wall* is the imaginary barrier between the stage and the audience. When actors say "don't cross the fourth wall," they mean that actors shouldn't comment on the action that's unfolding on stage. In linguistics, these reflective comments on an ongoing conversation are called *metacommunication* because they communicate about communication. In almost all cases—including in everyday conversation—metacommunication is highly constraining and generally removes the possibility for collaborative improvisation. In classrooms, however, teachers need to guide the improvisation, and it can be a useful instructional strategy to step outside of the unfolding classroom improvisation to comment on the conversation. Teachers might need to metacommunicate when students aren't being good collaborators, when they aren't following the improv rules themselves. For example, a teacher might metacommunicate when a strong-willed student is "denying" fellow students. When the high school teacher Sara Allen started to give her students more control over the improvisational flow of the discussion, a few boys started to dominate the discussion and a lot of the other students felt excluded. Allen chose to metacommunicate with the students, guiding them to understand what they were doing, for example, by videotaping one discussion, showing it to the class, and asking them to analyze what was going on (Allen, 1992; Cazden, 2001, p. 84).

Teachers can metacommunicate to call attention to when the improvisation has led to an important subject-area insight. But it's hard to know exactly when is the best time to stop the class's improvisation. When an important insight emerges from the discussion, should you call attention to it immediately, so it can provide a basis for the discussion to move to the next level? Or should you make a note of it and then call attention to it at the end of the discussion period, so as to allow the discussion to continue on its natural path? This tension is an example of what I call the teaching paradox, and in Chapter 4 I'll provide techniques that can help you manage this paradox.

The best teachers, just like improv actors, are able to accomplish these metacommunicative goals indirectly, without interrupting the unfolding conversation, so that the classroom improvisation continues without interruption (Sawyer, 2003).

WHEN TEACHERS NEED TO BREAK THE RULES

In classrooms with guided improvisation the teacher doesn't improvise without the students, and the students don't improvise without the teacher. Guided improvisation involves everyone, both teacher and students, in collaborative, exploratory, and improvised discussion. In my analyses of improv theater, I call this *collaborative emergence* because the performance *emerges*, unpredictably, from the joint actions of everyone on stage (Sawyer, 2003, 2004a, 2015). The rules of improv are designed to push creativity and control away from the individual performer, toward the creativity of interaction among members of the group.

As teachers guide student improvisations, they shouldn't relinquish control to the same degree as improv actors. The teacher isn't "the sage on the stage," but even so, the teacher retains the responsibility and authority to "guide from the side." Even during the most improvised free-flowing discussion, you still need to keep in mind the day's lesson plan and curriculum goals. At the same time, if the constructivist benefits of collaborative discussion are to be realized, you can't "drive" the entire class session. Otherwise, there's no true improvisation, and the students are prevented from learning through their own creative process.

The most effective teachers are highly attentive at every moment of the discussion. Even though they are performing as a fellow actor in the classroom's improvisation, they also need to think like a theater director and monitor how the collective construction of creative knowledge emerges from the group discussion.

LESSON PLANNING FOR GUIDED IMPROVISATION

The most experienced teachers, who are skilled at guided improvisation, still develop lesson plans. Even with a decade or two of teaching experience, after you've improvised in just about every imaginable situation, it's just not possible to make everything up as you go along. But these experienced teachers, like Mr. Knight (discussed earlier in this chapter), approach curriculum planning in a very different way from what you read about in methods textbooks. Instead of planning for a scripted sequence of actions, expert teachers *plan for improvisation*. When you compare the lesson plans of beginning teachers to those of experienced teachers, the experts are more than twice as likely to design adaptable lesson plans (Housner & Griffey, 1985). Experienced teachers are also more likely to modify their plan on the spot when they notice an unexpected learning opportunity based on a student's comment (Borko & Livingston, 1989; Erickson, 1982; Mehan, 1979).[5]

The best plans guide student improvisations so that they follow a learning trajectory that emerges from their improvisations, but one that's designed to lead them to the intended learning outcome for the lesson. A *learning trajectory* (sometimes called a *learning progression*) is the path a learner takes from a starting point of not knowing, to an endpoint of having learned the intended learning outcome (Confrey, 2006; Cooper et al., 2015, page 281; Daro, Mosher, & Corcoran, 2011).

Learning scientists are working with cognitive psychologists to map out the conceptual pathways that result in the most effective student construction of creative knowledge. And it turns out that the optimal learning trajectory isn't a linear path from not-knowing to knowing. Instead, researchers have found that students learn more effectively when they follow a zig-zagging, improvisational path. In Figure 3.1, the student's improvisational knowledge construction is represented by the river. The riverbanks are the scaffolds that guide a student's improvisational learning pathway. The rocks are *obstacles*—common errors and dead ends that many students are likely to encounter during their improvisational learning process—and the *landmarks* are moments of cognitive stability, when the learner has partially learned, but hasn't yet attained the *learned ideas*, the complex conceptual structure and understanding associated with creative knowledge.

Learning trajectories research is new, and each new study provides us with exciting and practical advice. But we have enough research at this point to know that these trajectories are subject-specific and age-specific. Ideally, guided improvisation would lead students down a research-based learning trajectory that leads to curricular goals.

In instructionist classrooms, students typically follow a linear learning trajectory. A linear trajectory works well enough for teaching students shallow knowledge. They learn one chunk of knowledge after another in a

Figure 3.1. The Learning Trajectory

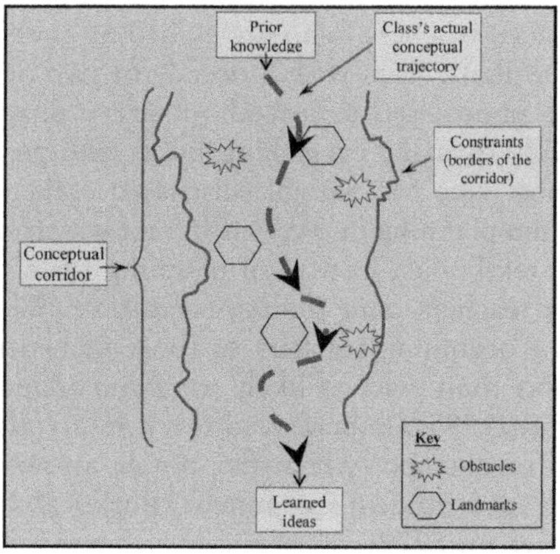

Note. From "The Evolution of Design Studies as Methodology" by J. Confrey, in R.K. Sawyer (Ed.), *The Cambridge Handbook of the Learning Sciences,* 2006 (pp. 135–151), New York, NY: Cambridge.

prescribed sequence. But when the learning goal is creative knowledge, students learn most effectively through a nonlinear but guided path. The river is wide, allowing student improvisations, while guiding them so that they don't end up in unproductive activities that are unrelated to the intended curricular goals.

BALANCING STRUCTURE AND IMPROVISATION

When planning a lesson, I recommend that teachers think in terms of scaffolds instead of scripts. Your plan should enable and guide student learning improvisations. But it can be hard to teach with just the right amount of structure and improvisation. A teacher might plan with too much structure, reducing the potential for improvisation; or a teacher might plan with too little structure, in which case the students may have fun and be creative, but without attaining the desired learning outcome.

Although both of these extremes reduce effective creative learning, it's much more common for a beginning teacher to use too much structure. That's natural because it's stressful to face uncertainty. Psychologists know that anxiety is a natural reaction to situations where you don't know what's going to happen. This anxiety is even more extreme for teachers because they're responsible for leading the students to curricular goals. Teachers want to be certain that their students will reach the required learning outcomes.

Even teachers at the most open and creative schools struggle with guided improvisation, and often plan with too much structure. Kevin Brookhouser at the York School has seen this with almost every new teacher:

> Having a clear curriculum eliminates some of the scary variables that face teachers, but I would argue passionately that we need to throw these boxes out the window. I do agree that there needs to be some structure. As for striking the balance between freedom and restriction, I don't know the exact balance. That's gonna vary based on the culture of the school and the individual students and the teacher. Personally, I would lean on the freedom. I'm always surprised at how letting go of more control produces more interesting results by my students. (Quoted in Creason, 2017)

Sarah Lasseter, a high school biology teacher in Durham, North Carolina, starts her fall semester with a guided improvisation activity that teaches the characteristics of life. First, she asks students to come up with their own ideas for what makes something living versus nonliving. Then, she shows them a box of objects, both living and nonliving, that she's prepared in advance. She asks them to apply their creative list of characteristics to the things in the box. As they categorize objects, they refine their list of characteristics. Then Lasseter asks them to focus only on their pile of living objects, and has them create a new list of the characteristics that they share. When everyone comes together for guided discussion, she responds to student questions. Many of their characteristics of life are wrong, and she guides them toward the scientifically accurate list that the students need to learn. She described the activity this way: "Students are doing the same thing that scientists, botanists, and naturalists do: They pose questions, test their hypotheses, analyze how their tentative list matches their observations, and then they iterate—continuously constructing and adapting their understanding based on observations" (Lasseter, personal communication).

SUMMARY

Guided improvisation is a practical application of constructivist and sociocultural learning theory. It's aligned with a large body of research showing that students learn creative knowledge most effectively when they actively participate in the classroom and when they construct their own knowledge. To construct knowledge, students need the freedom to engage in an open-ended improvisational process. Students can't learn creative knowledge from the predictability and linear structure of instructionism.

But we also know that the most effective learning happens when student knowledge construction is guided down a learning trajectory with appropriate scaffolds. It doesn't foster creativity to give students unconstrained freedom. In fact, some studies show that when students engage in unconstrained creative exercises, it actually *reduces* their creativity (Scott et al., 2004).

Guided improvisation is hard because teachers need to continually balance structure and improvisation. There's no rulebook to follow. In fact, I think that "rules" are the wrong way to think about effective creative teaching. I'm worried that any rulebook would miss the essence of guided improvisation. A rigid application of instructional strategies will prevent improvisation. Fortunately, the latest learning sciences research provides guidance in helping teachers design the optimum amount of guidance, as they face the teaching paradox: the challenge of balancing structure and freedom, constraint and improvisation. The next chapter provides techniques to help you master this paradox.

NOTES

1. Many other studies of teacher expertise find that experienced teachers improvise more (e.g., Nilssen, Gudmundsdottir, & Wangsmo-Cappelen, 1995; Sassi & Goldsmith, 1995; Sassi, Morse, & Goldsmith, 1997).

2. Other books that summarize the research showing that guided improvisation is the best way to teach are *Applying the Science of Learning* (Mayer, 2010) and *Education for Life and Work: Developing Transferable Knowledge and Skills in the 21st Century* (Pellegrino & Hilton, 2012).

3. This list of teacher behaviors that support student creativity is a combination of research findings from a large number of studies, including Craft, 2005; Cropley, 1997; Feldhusen & Treffinger, 1980; Fleith, 2000; Piirto, 2004; Rejskind, 2000; Sawyer, 2012; Sternberg & Williams, 1996; and Torrance, 1965, 1970.

4. Studies showing that the best teachers guide the class in a group improvisation include Bearison, Magzamen, & Filardo, 1986; Cobb, 1995; Doise & Mugny, 1984; and Perret-Clermont, 1980.

5. Many studies have found that the most effective classroom interaction balances structure and script, including Baker-Sennett & Matusov, 1997; Borko & Livingston, 1989; Brown & Edelson, 2001; Erickson, 1982; Mehan, 1979; Rogoff, 1998; Simon, 1995; and Yinger, 1987.

CHAPTER 4

Mastering the Teaching Paradox

The best way to teach for creative knowledge is with guided improvisation. Students have freedom to improvisationally explore the subject area, enabling them to construct their own knowledge. But we also know that student knowledge construction is more effective when their classroom improvisations are guided. How can you balance structure with improvisation? I call this the *teaching paradox*. It's a paradox because there's no single, perfect way to balance structure and improvisation. Every classroom, every grade, and every subject will need a different balance. You've probably already noticed that this book doesn't offer detailed classroom methods to use for a specific grade or a specific subject. Of course, you can find a lot of methods textbooks that are designed just for your subject, that give you very specific classroom techniques. These books give you important advice about how to teach in ways that are specific to your subject. But, to my mind, many of these books are overly scripted. They rarely tell you how to guide classroom improvisations, or how to plan in ways that accommodate, and foster, guided improvisation. I think that's why so many studies of teacher expertise find that as teachers grow from beginner to expert, they increasingly leave these textbook methods behind: it's because they gradually learn, from practice and experience, how to guide improvisation. As you grow in expertise, you'll be less reliant on scripts and plans, and you'll be increasingly comfortable with improvisation. In every class and every semester you become increasingly skilled at resolving the teaching paradox in a way that's most appropriate for your own subject, grade level, and teaching style.

I start this chapter by providing some general principles that work in every subject to help you succeed with the teaching paradox. These general principles can help you develop lesson plans and instructional strategies that guide classroom improvisations so that students learn creative knowledge and you reach your curricular goals. In the second half of the chapter, I describe six different successful and influential learning environments that balance the teaching paradox in different ways—ranging from the Exploratorium, a legendary science center in San Francisco, to *orchestration scripts*, educational software designs that guide students through a very scripted path that still provides a small space for improvisation.

Teaching with guided improvisation is hard; it's much harder than teaching with instructionism. To guide student improvisations, you have to master a repertoire of routines—short, scripted bits of classroom interaction that can provide in-the-moment guidance. (Methods textbooks tend to focus on these routines.) But in addition, you have to be able to use these routines improvisationally, flexibly, and opportunistically. To balance structure and improvisation, teachers face two related challenges:

- *The challenge for classroom practice.* Teachers need to enable and support student improvisations, but also provide structure that guides them toward creative knowledge that meets their curricular goals. With increasing experience, teachers will master a repertoire of plans, routines, and structures, and they'll be able to use these adaptively to guide classroom improvisations.
- *The challenge for curriculum design.* Classroom improvisations are more effective when teachers develop lesson plans to guide each class. These advance plans help to guide students most effectively toward creative knowledge. But these plans can't be applied rigidly, like a script. Lesson plans should be flexible enough to allow for classroom improvisation.

In Chapter 3 I described research showing that students learn better when the lesson plan provides some structure that guides their learning trajectory. But at the same time, students need to feel comfortable improvising. You don't want the students to sit back and wait for you to tell them what to do. Compared to their passive role in instructionism, in guided improvisation students explore the unknown. They ask new questions. They work on problems that they don't yet know how to solve.

In creative classrooms these two challenges are addressed through the artful dance of guided improvisation. In Chapter 3 I called this dance *collaborative emergence*, because the flow of the class session *emerges* from a joint performance between the teacher and the students. Fortunately, the cutting edge of learning sciences research and practice is focused on exactly these challenges. The teaching paradox is faced, to some degree, by all constructivist teaching—because if students are scripted down a linear path, then they aren't given the chance to construct their own knowledge. And, in fact, many people use the same language to describe creative teaching that they use when describing good teaching (Kind & Kind, 2007).

The solution to the teaching paradox is to design scaffolds that guide students through a learning trajectory—a conceptual path that leads a student most effectively toward creative knowledge. In the last chapter, in Figure 3.1, I represented a learning trajectory as a river, twisting and turning around bends, flowing past rocks (common misconceptions) and landmarks (partial understandings that lead learning forward). Scaffolds are the banks of the river: structures that guide students. When well designed, these structures don't overly limit student creativity; paradoxically, they enable students to improvise their learning more effectively.

The best balance between classroom structures and student improvisations will change with the grade level you're teaching, and with the student's own location and path in their learning trajectory. The balance will change depending on your learning goals for the class session. And you can adapt the balance to work best with your own teaching style. In this chapter, to help you think about the best balance for your own class, I describe six different learning environments—including schools, science centers, makerspaces, and educational software—each of which demonstrates a different balance. The first of the six—the San Francisco Exploratorium—has a low degree of structure. The last—orchestration scripts—has a very high degree of structure. They all enable some amount of student improvisation, from a large amount of freedom to very little freedom. Each of the six has been studied by learning scientists, and we've demonstrated that they all guide students toward creative knowledge in different ways that are matched to the subject, the level of the students, and the intended learning outcomes. These examples show you a variety of ways to think about how to balance structure and improvisation, and find a balance that's best aligned with your own classroom needs.

The teaching paradox never goes away because the optimal balance of structure and freedom keeps changing depending on where students are in their learning trajectory. In this chapter, my goal is to help you think about how to continuously manage this balance in response to each student and each class.

THE STRUCTURES OF GUIDED IMPROVISATION

When a construction crew starts work on a new building, they put up scaffolding, a temporary, lightweight frame that surrounds the building as it rises up. The scaffolding supports the workers and material needed as the building rises. This is a wonderful metaphor for guided improvisation: The students need guiding, temporary structures at first, to help them "construct" their own creative knowledge. Creative knowledge—as I showed in Chapter 2—is big, complex, and profound. You can't learn it all at once; you learn it through a guided process. Instructionism is very different: When you teach small, superficial knowledge, students learn one small thing at a time. They don't need scaffolding, because instructionist teaching is like throwing bricks on top of a pile. Students are simply acquiring a longer list of tiny chunks of knowledge. But to learn creative knowledge, students need support. It takes time and effort to build knowledge that's big, complex, connected, and integrated. In a creative classroom, the teacher provides scaffolding for the students, because they aren't able to understand the big picture right way. The scaffolding supports them as they develop creative knowledge until they've reached a point where their understanding is big, connected, and networked.

Once a building is finished, the builders dismantle the scaffolds. In the same way, once a student has constructed creative knowledge, the classroom scaffolds are no longer necessary. At the end of the learning trajectory, their knowledge is a complex conceptual system, able to stand on its own. At this point, the teacher *fades* the scaffold. "Fading" is a process where the teacher monitors the classroom's progress, and in response, carefully and slowly removes the guiding structures, as students gain more and more understanding.

When students first encounter new material, they need a lot of scaffolding. At this point, you should emphasize structure because the students aren't yet ready for open-ended improvisation. As students move through the learning trajectory, they construct increasingly complex and complete knowledge, and the teacher can fade these structures. As classroom structures fade, classroom activities gradually become more improvisational. At the end of the learning trajectory, when students have reached your curricular goals and mastered the creative knowledge of that unit, they're able to create with that knowledge. They no longer need the scaffolds.

During creative learning, the optimum balance between structure and improvisation continually evolves. Because guided improvisation allows students to take their own paths, the teacher needs to guide each student in the specific way that matches their own current understanding. Students learn better when their learning improvisations are guided with constant and immediate feedback all through the learning process.

These moments of feedback are called *formative assessments*. Formative assessment is a flexible, continuously unfolding awareness of what students know, with the purpose of shaping the learning trajectory. Unlike *summative assessments*—the high-stakes tests that students take at the end of a school year—formative assessments are designed *for the student*, to guide their learning improvisations.

Expert teachers are better at improvising with students, but paradoxically, they also have a bigger repertoire of *routines* than novice teachers (see Chapter 3). Routines are standard sequences of actions, responses to students, guiding questions or prompts, or short breakouts for group discussion. These routines can be very effective at scaffolding classroom improvisations. Some examples include:

- Short conversational exchanges that come up often. For example, you may have developed an effective way to guide a student through a temporary mistake that you've learned is fairly common.

- A short 5-minute activity that you can use in response to an un-expected student question, when that question is similar to others you've been asked before.
- Short group activities, such as Think-Pair-Share: In response to a teacher question, each student writes down an answer; then they turn to another classmate to discuss each of these ideas; finally, each pair shares what they talked about with the rest of the class.
- Ways to link today's unexpected student questions and discoveries with material that's not scheduled until later in the semester. For example, you may have an opportunity to link today's learning goal with next week's unit, even though you haven't prepared for it yet.

Experienced teachers have developed an impressive number of routines. But they don't apply them using fixed rules. They spontaneously decide to use a routine when it supports the specific needs of that moment. And they apply each routine in a creative, improvisational fashion, not as a rigid script (Berliner, 1987; Leinhardt & Greeno, 1986). In the most effective classrooms, teachers balance structure and script with flexibility and im-provisation (Borko & Livingston, 1989; Brown & Edelson, 2001; Erickson, 1982; Gershon, 2006; Mehan, 1979; Simon, 1995; Yinger, 1987). The teachers don't parrot these scripts in exactly the same way every time; they improvise around their routines, in the same way that a jazz pianist impro-vises variations on the melody of a famous popular song (Berliner, 1987; Leinhardt & Greeno, 1986).

AGING GRACEFULLY

At Kansas State University, anthropologist Michael Wesch teaches the course "The anthropology of aging." The course is centered around a final semester project, where students create an educational videogame that al-lows players to think about decisions people face near the end of life—either for your aging parent or for yourself. Students read scholarship on aging (pharmacology and neurobiology), how different societies treat their elderly (anthropology), game design and aesthetics (design thinking and narrative structure), and complex coding (computer science). And on top of that, students leave their dorms for the entire term and move into a local retirement community. They see and talk with aging residents, and also with their care providers and even the housekeepers (Davidson, 2017).

In designing and building their own videogame, there's no question that students are engaging in a creative process. And yet, that creative pro-cess is guided by many structures provided by the teacher: the parameters of the assignment itself, the readings and concepts provided by the teacher, the teacher's advice about how to talk with residents, and guidance about how to gather observational data that they'll use in their game design.

PROJECT-BASED LEARNING AND THE TEACHING PARADOX

Project-based learning (PBL) has great potential for fostering creative learning. It's a research-based type of guided improvisation; PBL units are designed with a loose structure that guides students through a learning trajectory. Research on PBL provides a lot of information about exactly how to design a good project assignment and how to plan for improvisation (Krajcik & Shin, 2014).

A PBL unit starts with an *open-ended problem*. The best open-ended problems are designed with some ambiguity about how to proceed, and that ambiguity is an essential part of the learning experience. But dealing with ambiguity is a challenge for both students and teachers. When a teacher first tries PBL, they often try to reduce this ambiguity by assigning problems that are too specific to allow for guided improvisation. When an assignment is too specific, students don't learn for creativity, because they can solve the problem by taking a linear path toward the correct solution. When a problem statement is very specific, it's called a *well-structured problem*: one where students know, right after they receive the assignment, where they'll end up and what their design or solution will look like (see Table 4.1). Then they follow a linear and predictable path to their solution.

KING MIDDLE SCHOOL IN PORTLAND, MAINE

King Middle School has a student population that's 60% low-income. Twenty-two percent of the students are refugees for whom English is a second language. For years, student test scores were below the state achievement average. So the school's teachers and leaders decided on a dramatic transformation to project-based learning (PBL). After the school redesigned their curriculum around PBL, the students began to outscore the state average on 6 of 7 subjects; in some subjects, they were in the top third.

The curriculum was transformed to foster guided improvisation. Students worked on 4- to 12-week interdisciplinary projects at least twice each year. These projects included:

- An aquarium design judged by local architects
- A CD narrative of the Walt Whitman poem "O Captain! My Captain!" by ESL students
- Writing a book called *Voices of U.S.* (a collection of immigrant stories)
- A guide to the shore life of nearby Casco Bay
- Documentaries on learning with laptop computers
- A claymation video explaining Newton's laws of motion

(Darling-Hammond et al., 2008, pp. 40–41)

Table 4.1. Well-Structured Problems versus Open-Ended Problems

Well-structured problems	Open-ended problems
All of the facts needed to solve the problem are presented to students.	Some problem elements are unknown or uncertain.
The goal is clearly stated and students know exactly what they're supposed to do.	The goal is vaguely defined or unclear.
The relevant parameters and constraints are specified explicitly.	Some important constraints aren't explicit and have to be discovered along the way.
The rules and principles needed to solve the problem are listed.	The necessary rules aren't provided, and students need to figure out what's necessary.
There is one correct solution.	There are multiple possible solutions.
There's a linear path to the solution, and students can tell how close they are to finishing.	There are many possible solution paths, and it can be hard to tell how far along you are.

Note. Adapted from "Towards a Design Theory of Problem Solving," by D. H. Jonassen, 2000, *Educational Technology, Research, and Development, 48*(4), pp. 63–85.

PBL only leads to creative knowledge when the problem is open-ended. Open-ended problems require students to engage in many of the creative habits of mind in Chapter 2: asking good questions, being mindfully aware of possibly relevant information, occasionally encountering dead ends or failures, and experimenting and iterating through the solution path. When solving an open-ended problem, students often take a path that's unpredictable, ambiguous, and uncertain.

But "open ended" doesn't mean a complete absence of structure. In PBL classrooms, students need a lot of scaffolding—in the form of parameters and constraints—to successfully work through an open-ended problem. In my studies of how professors teach in design schools, I discovered that design education uses a unique type of PBL, and that their problems—while open-ended—still have a lot of scaffolding (Sawyer, 2018b). For example, Figure 4.1 is a project that was assigned in Professor Heather Corcoran's MFA class on Communication Design at Washington University in St. Louis. You'll see that Corcoran provides quite a bit of structure to guide the students' creative thinking and acting. Why does she assign a novel to each student, and why is it from this specific list of five novels? You might think that students would be more creative if they were allowed to select any novel on their own. But Corcoran, a veteran teacher with over 15 years of experience, has learned that students are *more* creative with these advance

Figure 4.1. A Project Assignment in a Communication Design Class

diptych broadsides: beginnings & endings

Assignment

Each of you has been assigned a novel. You will design two broadside/posters in which you display a short text from the beginning and a short text from the ending in the most visually dynamic way possible. You may use images, or not.

Your posters should function as interesting companions. This is an opportunity for visual—and more specifically, typographic—risk. What is the relationship between expressive type and communicative value?

Your process should involve a wide range of solutions. Given. But it should also involve a distinct set of entry points into the problem.

Your first body of evidence should include:

I. Read and select.
Read or reread your novel. Think about its story arc, meaning and use of language. Think about how the beginning and ending frame the novel.

Select two passages of no more than 100 words each from the first few pages and last few pages of your novel. You may not eliminate any text between the first and last words of your passages. Your job is to select, interpret, and express, but not to write or edit.

2. Collect examples.
This should include examples of expressive type in the world that may or may not relate to your text, as well as examples of posters are other surface design that uses type expressively. How are people borrowing and manipulating letterforms? How might you adapt their ideas and methods?

3. Find visual material.
Collect images or other visual material related to your texts. Go for variety and volume.

4. Make visual sketches.
Sketches of potential approaches to the broadside. Worry less about pairings, initially, and more about volume, ideas, and range of formal approaches.

Novels

Willa Cather: *My Antonia*
Dave Eggers: *You Shall Know Our Velocity*
Cormac McCarthy: *All the Pretty Horses*
Zora Neale Hurston: *Their Eyes Were Watching God*
Michael Cunningham: *The Hours*

Criteria

Each of your posters must include your assigned text so that it can be read, the name of your book, the author, and the year.

16x20 inches

Posters must be output on one surface. Image, color, type unlimited.

structures. Another professor, the illustrator John Hendrix, told me "a good project has severe constraints. Constraints are actually setting you free" (Sawyer, 2018b, p. 156).

Studies show that when students engage in PBL, their motivation is higher than in an instructionist classroom (Darling-Hammond et al., 2008, p. 42). Motivation increases even more for students who haven't done well in traditional instructionist classrooms. For example, PBL has been shown to be particularly effective for students with learning disabilities. In one study, elementary kids with learning disabilities benefited more than any other students from a shift to PBL (Xin et al., 2017). This is a big deal, because students with special needs are underrepresented in STEM (Israel, Maynard, & Williamson, 2013; National Science Foundation, NCSES, 2013). To date, only a few schools have used problem-based learning with students with cognitive and learning disabilities. The reason is that it's widely believed that these students learn best from *direct instruction*—a pedagogy that's even more scripted and rigid than a traditional instructionist classroom. But most research shows that PBL works better than scripted instruction (Belland, Walker, & Kim, 2017).

MANAGING THE TEACHING PARADOX: SIX CASE STUDIES

The best balance of structure and improvisation will vary with every grade, every learning outcome and state standard, and with every class. There's no magic bullet to resolve the teaching paradox. This is the challenge of teaching for creativity: It's always improvisational, the improvisations are always structured, and the balance is always changing.

Here are six case studies of how innovative educators have not only managed the teaching paradox, but have used it constructively to drive creative learning. The first case study has the most improvisation and least structure, and the last one has the least improvisation and the most structure. In all six, students develop creative knowledge, even though the amount of scaffolding varies dramatically.

Example 1. Exploration and Inquiry: The San Francisco Exploratorium

In the summer of 2009 I spent a month at the San Francisco Exploratorium. The Exploratorium, founded in 1969, was the first interactive science center. Visitors are encouraged to touch, to modify, and to experiment with the exhibits. While interacting with exhibits, visitors engage in a process of inquiry that introduces them to scientific thinking (Cole, 2009; Sawyer, 2015). This process of open-ended inquiry encourages visitors to engage in many of the creative practices described in Chapter 2, such as asking good questions, experimenting, and being mindfully aware of what might happen.

Each Exploratorium exhibit captures a natural phenomenon in a way that reveals the beauty of nature, the aesthetic aspect of the natural world. A good exhibit presents a human-scale phenomenon that can be experienced in a minute or two. A simple example is the Balancing Ball, where a tube shoots out a narrow stream of air, and a beach ball floats in the stream, without falling down (see Figure 4.2). The visitor experiences the phenomenon in an intimate, immediate way. It's compelling and engaging, and visitors want to learn more. This fosters a mindset of inquiry—the same motivation that drives scientists to explore, discover, analyze, and explain the world.

Many exhibit developers are scientists themselves. They know that the scientific process is creative, iterative, and improvisational. Their goal is to create exhibits where visitors are scaffolded through this same unpredictable and exploratory process. As visitors interact and explore, they engage in a creative process of inquiry—asking new questions, being aware and observant, and iteratively experimenting with the phenomenon. Visitors will take different learning paths as they interact with an exhibit. Each visitor might learn something different from an exhibit. The developers embrace this uncertainty; they couldn't be happier when a visitor learns something that they didn't anticipate. After all, they reason, this is also the process of inquiry that working scientists pursue. These exhibits encourage visitors to think like scientists—following a creative process driven by curiosity and inquiry, a process that can lead to the discovery of new knowledge.

For these reasons, the Exploratorium's approach to guided improvisation is relatively unscaffolded. They don't design a lesson plan or a learning trajectory. Their approach to the teaching paradox is to encourage the learner's improvisation, with as little structure as possible. The Exploratorium shows one way to approach the teaching paradox: Focus on creative improvisation and open-ended exploration rather than scaffolds, teacher guidance, or standard learning outcomes. Teachers love to take their students on field trips to the Exploratorium. They can see their students getting excited about science. Creative teachers understand the importance of the inquiry mindset, and science teachers know that hands-on exploration in science supports creativity. Curiosity and inquiry are at the core of scientific creativity. After all, scientists don't simply discover new facts, as if they are passive observers of the world. They do that, to be sure. But if all that science gave us were more facts, we'd just have an increasingly long list of shallow knowledge. Along with new facts, science continually advances our understanding of the world with creative knowledge: deep, connected, and adaptable.

As you design lesson plans and problem-based assignments, you can borrow the most effective feature of the Exploratorium's approach: fostering student improvisational learning. The challenge is to add structure to

Figure 4.2. The Balancing Ball Exhibit

these motivating, inquiry-inspiring experiences, but without removing the potential to inspire improvisational action.

When I interviewed some Exploratorium staff, they told me that school educators frequently ask how each of their exhibits aligns with California state science standards. If you don't know what students are going to learn from a particular exhibit, then how are you going to weave this field trip into the content that you're teaching at that point in the school year? But exhibit developers are faithful to the authentic creative process of science, where scientists are exploring the world, not knowing what answers they'll get or even if they're asking the right question.

The Exploratorium exhibit designers are incredibly good at what they do; they've intentionally decided to provide minimal structure for visitors. The inquiry mindset experienced by Exploratorium visitors provides us with a new way to think about how to approach guided improvisation. Compared to just about all other learning environments, the Exploratorium probably has the least structure. It has been influential among science educators because it suggests that science learning can happen even when students are given almost complete freedom.

Example 2. Scaffolding the Science Center Experience: EdVentures

The Exploratorium's innovative approach has influenced science centers in the United States and around the world. They're inspired by the Exploratorium's success in engaging visitors in scientific inquiry, in observing the world scientifically, and in bringing together art, design, and exploration. But most other science centers provide more scaffolding around the visitor's learning process. They often start out their exhibit design process by focusing on an intended learning outcome, one that's aligned with state standards. Then they design a series of exhibits to align with these curricular goals (Serrell, 1996).

For example, EdVenture, a science center and makerspace in Columbia, South Carolina, offers programs for grades K–8, where on-staff educators guide students to learn specific science content from their exhibits. The programs are structured in ways that align with a list of South Carolina state standards. On their website, each program is advertised along with the matching list of learning outcomes in their *School Program Guide* (EdVenture, 2017)). Here's one example of the structure of a program that's provided for teachers to help them design their class curriculum in ways that align with the field trip:

Zap! Electricity at Work

- Grades: 3–5
- Subject: Physical Science
- Size and length: 30 student max per 45 minute session
- Led by: An EdVentures staff educator
- SC Standards: Science 3.S.1, 3.P.3, 3.P.3A

What is electricity? How will our world be without it? Students will learn about the atomic model, the flow of electrons, types of electricity, circuits and how to be safe around electricity. They will participate in fun Van der Graaf demonstrations, create a human circuit, see how a magnetic field can generate electricity and observe a pickle being zapped. (p. 11)

Many teachers welcome the scaffolding provided at EdVenture because it's easier to integrate student activities with their curricular goals—in the way that the "Zap!" program helps teachers accomplish curricular goals that are aligned with the state's required electronics standards.

Example 3. Learning Through Making

Makerspaces are popping up all over the country. Imagine a blend of shop class, home economics, art studios, and science labs. Children engage in hands-on activities, such as cooking, sewing, welding, robotics, painting, printing, or building. The goal is to design and make something tangible through a creative and iterative process—helping students develop the creative mindsets of Chapter 2.

Makerspaces can be as simple as rooms filled with plastic straws, old cardboard boxes, and craft supplies, like the Scrap Exchange in Durham, North Carolina (www.scrapexchange.org). Or they can be packed with cool technologies, like 3-D printers, programmable robots, and virtual reality goggles, like the ImagineLab at the University of North Carolina's School of Education (ccee.unc.edu/summercamp/). The ImagineLab gives children small, inexpensive toys and robots that can be "programmed" using a visual, drag-and-drop smartphone app that's easy enough for children as young as 5 or 6. Unlike sitting at a computer and writing code, these programs are concrete and tangible. They have an impact on the world that you can see.

Both the Exploratorium and makerspaces draw inspiration from the influential constructivist theories of Piaget, Dewey, Froebel, and Montessori. These progressive educators argued for the importance of active learning through concrete, creative activities. Maker activities are good models for guided improvisation because they incorporate several features that researchers have associated with deep learning for creative knowledge:

- *Learning is embodied.* Learners physically interact with external artifacts. Their bodies, senses, and hands are fully engaged. Research has found that when learning activities involve the body, learning for creative knowledge is more effective (Abrahamson & Lindgren, 2014).
- *Knowledge is externalized.* In making, a learner's unfolding knowledge is visible in the external object. This helps students develop *metacognition,* the ability to reflect on their own developing understandings. Research has found that metacognitive skill increases a learner's ability to learn deep knowledge (Winne & Azevedo, 2014).
- *Students are intrinsically motivated.* In a survey of hundreds of hobbyist makers—model rocketeers, home brewers, motorcycle racers, musicians—they said they loved what they were doing. They weren't doing it for a grade or to impress anyone (Pfaffman, 2003). Psychologists call this *intrinsic motivation,* and research shows that creative learning is more likely when learners are intrinsically motivated (Järvelä & Renninger, 2014). When people make things, they're more motivated than they are in school. There's almost nothing more motivating than making something you can see and touch (Pfaffman, 2003). When students are asked, "What did you like about your favorite class?" and they could pick any class they'd taken, they almost always describe activities where they could physically see what they had learned. Maker activities can contribute to learning in any subject; these students mentioned classes in all subjects, from music, to English language arts, to math.

Most maker activities happen outside of classrooms, in after-school clubs or in science centers. Makerspaces are rarely designed to lead to specific school learning outcomes. Most makerspaces balance the teaching paradox like the Exploratorium does: They support student improvisational knowledge construction but provide very little structure. In fact, the Exploratorium has its own makerspace, The Tinkering Studio (www.

exploratorium.edu/tinkering/), which has developed activities that are now used in makerspaces all over the country. But can be difficult for teachers to integrate maker activities into the required curriculum.

Like teachers, when parents take their kids to a makerspace on a weekend, they're not always sure what to do with the dramatic range of possibilities. When parents visit a makerspace with their child, they often guide their child to make a specific object, one that's nice enough to take home and display for relatives and visitors. They want their child to be proud of their invention, and hope that their success might stimulate their interest in science and engineering. The invention they take home is a memory of their day together.

Jarrett Grimm-Vavlitis, manager of the makerspace at Kidzu Children's Museum in Chapel Hill, North Carolina, told me that this is pretty common: Parents often focus on what the end product will look like, rather than guide their child through an iterative, unpredictable design process. But children learn creativity better when they make something that looks like a complete mess. It will probably fall apart in the car on the way home, and after a few days it may not be worth keeping. Sometimes it can be better to sign up for a scheduled workshop with a trained educator, who can encourage children to learn from iterative design, failure, and experimentation in an environment where failure is embraced, rather than avoided.

Example 4. Scaffolding Maker and Museum Activities in the Classroom

Many schools are adapting the freedom and creativity of maker and museum activities by adding some degree of additional structure that guides these improvisations toward creative knowledge that's aligned with curricular goals.

Take a look at Figure 4.3 to see two different ways to structure the same maker activity. In this activity, students make an object that they put into a wind tube. One museum used the variation on the left of Figure 4.3, and didn't specify a goal for the task. They allowed students to decide what they want to do. A second museum gave students the same activity, but modified it as displayed on the right side of Figure 4.3: they suggested that visitors work within these parameters: "Make an object that will hover between these two lines." The version that you choose will depend on how specific your learning goals are for the exhibit.

When schools use makerspace activities, it's usually integrated with a project-based learning unit. This combination of making and PBL has great potential to support learning for creative knowledge. Earlier in this chapter, I described research showing that students learn more from PBL when they're guided by right kinds of questions, parameters, and goals. For example, one study compared two groups of students as they built model rockets (Petrosino, 1998; also see Schwartz, Tsang, & Blair, 2016, p. 157). One

Figure 4.3. Two Variations of a Maker Exhibit

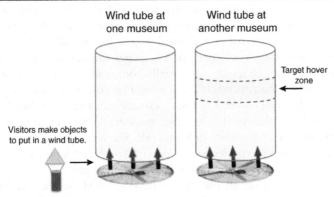

Note. The variation on the right gives visitors an optional goal; the one at the left allows visitors complete freedom to define their own goal. From *The ABCs of How We Learn: 26 Scientifically Proven Approaches, How They Work, and When to Use Them* (p. 157), by D. L. Schwartz, J. M. Tsang, and K. P. Blair, 2016, New York, NY: Norton.

group of students did the standard activity, while a second group was given an additional goal: "Create a design plan that NASA can use with its new model rocket kit." These students were also asked to test certain specific features of their rockets and see their effect on flight, including the number of fins, and what paint they used. When both groups were later asked, "What was the purpose of this activity?" the first group said, "To build rockets." They'd learned only shallow knowledge. In contrast, the second group had developed creative knowledge. They could say quite a bit about the specific physics principles they'd learned, and they could tell that learning deeper physics concepts was the teacher's goal for the activity.

The model rocket study, and many others like it, show that students often learn creative knowledge better when you add structure to open-ended activities. This additional structure is particularly important for teachers who need to guide students toward particular curricular goals. But it's important to be careful in how you structure these activities. When schools first introduce making or inquiry to the classroom, it's all too common for them to impose too much structure. I've heard some people say that making and inquiry activities won't work in school because they're incompatible with curricular goals and mandatory assessments. But research like this shows how it can be done (Halverson & Sheridan, 2014).

Example 5. Scaffolding Making in the Classroom: FUSE Studio

Today, schools all over the country are successfully integrating making into their curriculum by using guided improvisation. One wonderful success story is the Eagle Lake School District (Stevens et al., 2018). Eagle Lake developed a maker-based curriculum that uses guided improvisation so that student making leads to required science learning outcomes. One girl, Kira, designed a fidget spinner using 3-D modeling software called TinkerCad, and then printed it using a 3-D printer. The fidget spinner actually worked! Other kids saw it, they thought it was really cool, and they asked Kira how to do it. Kira was proud to teach them how. Her role as a knowledgeable maker and teacher empowered her as a creator. Kira said, "Like, I never imagined I could do this stuff." Another student, Cecilia, created and designed a new utopian community in Minecraft. She was equally empowered, describing her learning experience this way: "You learn how to . . . overcome obstacles, so there's different kinds of learning I guess."

Eagle Lake was using an innovative new STEAM (science, technology, engineering, the arts, and mathematics) curriculum called FUSE Studio, which has been adopted by over 130 schools in Finland and in the United States (www.fusestudio.net). FUSE includes 30 STEAM challenge sequences that "level up" like videogames. These 30 challenges include programming a robot and building a dream home in 3-D. FUSE adds a lot of scaffolding to maker activities. But even with a lot of structure, some people are skeptical at first. Some thought these activities weren't structured enough. Some science teachers didn't even think this was a science class; one said, "I don't see a lot of science in this." From their perspective, what scientific knowledge do you need to design and print a fidget spinner? When you build a world in Minecraft, a critic might ask, "What science principles do you learn?" But these concerns are focused on shallow knowledge and coverage of material. FUSE is designed to teach core, crosscutting, underlying concepts of science and inquiry, like *patterns* and *cause and effect*: creative knowledge rather than shallow knowledge. FUSE engages students in the same inquiry mindset of open-ended inquiry as the Exploratorium. But it adds in structures that guide the learning trajectory. FUSE demonstrates that guided improvisation can be more effective than unstructured play and exploration. In Chapter 5 I expand on the lessons of the FUSE project to give recommendations for how to introduce guided improvisation in the classroom in ways that align with curriculum and assessment and standards.

Example 6. Structuring Improvisation with Orchestration Scripts

When schools first bring new technologies into the classroom—whether educational software, tablet apps, or Internet-based tools—teachers find it easiest to continue teaching essentially the same way. For example, they might insert the new technology wherever it seems most effective at supporting their existing lesson plan or classroom activity. But when new technology is wrapped into existing pedagogy, it rarely has much impact on student learning. And then, when student test scores stay the same, it can seem like you wasted a lot of money on shiny new toys. But the real potential of new educational technologies is to support a transformation from instructionism to creative classrooms. It requires a change in the way you think about lesson planning and instructional strategies. If you keep teaching the same way—if you're doing the same thing with technology that you used to do with pencil and paper—then, yes, buying computers is a waste of money.

Some schools add maker activities, but they do it by adding a new class period, and they put the materials and technologies in a separate room. This is the easiest way to bring making into a school because it isolates these new activities apart from the rest of the school day. In every other class, and every other period, the pedagogy stays the same. Throughout this book, I've shown you that creativity training works best if you integrate it into every class and every subject. It's the same way with making: Students won't learn creative knowledge from it if every subject continues to be taught the same traditional way. Deep, transformative change is hard. It can be a challenge when teachers first learn to teach in ways that take advantage of the potential of new technologies. But the principles of guided improvisation can help. When teachers first start to use technology to teach with guided improvisation, it helps for these new lesson plans to be relatively structured (Dimitriadis, 2012).

When groups of students collaborate on a project, structure can be particularly helpful. Research finds that collaboration can be challenging for students, and that without guiding structures, project groups are often ineffective (see Chapter 3). Some recent innovations in *computer-supported collaborative learning* (CSCL) can give some insight into how technologies can support collaborative classroom improvisations. These new CSCL experiments are designed to scaffold the team's collaborative dynamics, making it easier for students to learn from collaboration (Stahl, Koschmann, & Suthers, 2014).

To help teachers transform their teaching for these new technologies, some cutting-edge software is designed with *orchestration scripts* for teachers, which provide them with the structures they need to manage the many new variables in the classroom.[1] An *orchestration script* is a lesson plan containing a sequence of well-designed activities, such as small-group discussion and individual work. An orchestration script also includes instructional strategies—the "routines" I described earlier—that teachers can use at specific points in the lesson.

The first developers of orchestration scripts soon encountered the teaching paradox. The good news was that the scripts increased teacher effectiveness at using new technologies. The bad news was that the scripts were too structured, and students weren't able to improvisationally construct their own creative knowledge. That's why the cutting edge of today's research is exploring how to introduce improvisational flexibility while retaining the benefits of scripting to support teachers.

In the rural town of Cigales, Spain, the Ana de Austria primary school had introduced many new technologies for teachers, including digital white boards, tablet PCs, and software such as Group Scribbles (Dimitriadis, 2012). A team of researchers from the nearby University of Valladolid studied how teachers orchestrate classroom improvisations with students ages 6 to 8. Their goal was to better understand how to design orchestration scripts in ways that enable student improvisation within the structure.

The researchers started by watching a few class sessions to see how teachers balanced the teaching paradox. In one class, on a simple arithmetic lesson, the teacher used a lot of guiding structures, but left some openings for student improvisation. The teacher's balance of structure and creativity was so sophisticated that the researchers had to create a complex graphic tool to capture the flow of the classroom. Figure 4.4 shows the learning trajectory of one math class, using visual conventions that display the teacher's structured lesson plan, as well as her improvisations within that plan (Dimitriadis, 2012). The items in boldface weren't written into the lesson plan; they emerged from the classroom's improvisations. The figure is pretty complicated, but don't worry about the specific details. Just take a quick glance at what's in boldface, and you'll see that the class mostly unfolded just the way the teacher planned it. The unplanned improvisational moments—in boldface—are relatively small embellishments.

To help teachers develop lesson plans that incorporate technology while at the same time increasing the potential for improvisation, the research team created a professional development (PD) workshop. They used process maps like Figure 4.4 to help teachers reflect on their own practice, and they led a discussion about how the class session balanced structure and improvisation. The results were convincing: The PD workshop helped teachers become more effective at balancing the teaching paradox. They became more comfortable with improvising in response to the flow of the class. They were able to develop more flexible plans that allowed for improvisation.

It might seem counterintuitive, but the introduction of the orchestration script actually gave the teachers confidence to improvise more (Prieto, Villagrá-Sobrino, et al., 2011, p. 1224; also see Prieto, Dlab, Gutiérrez, Abdulwahed, & Balid, 2011). As I showed in Chapter 3 it's typical for teachers to be anxious when they first try guided improvisation because it's hard to predict how or when students will reach the intended learning outcomes. The researchers helped the teachers design scripts that reduced the uncertainty of the class's flow, allowing teachers to improvise with more confidence in the open parts of the script. These scripts acted as scaffolds for the teacher's own improvisational learning: As teachers gained experience with an orchestration script, they became increasingly likely to diverge from the lesson plan's script. The researchers began to see more improvisation in each class, as teachers combined different instructional routines and invented new ones on the fly.

Figure 4.4. An Orchestration Script in a Math Class

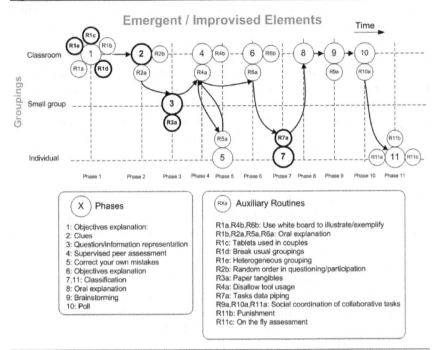

Note. From "Supporting Teachers in Orchestrating CSCL Classrooms," by Y. A. Dimitriadis, in A. Jimoyiannis (Ed.), *Research on E-Learning and ICT in Education* (p. 79), 2012, New York, NY: Springer.

Compared to the examples of guided improvisation throughout this book, Figure 4.4 looks extremely structured. And in fact, new research confirms that these scripts need to be more flexible. For example, scripts should be designed so that they can "fade" as teachers gain more experience with the lesson plan. In the study of the Ana de Austria school in Cigales, Spain, researchers found that experienced teachers improvised more—confirming the research findings I described in Chapter 3 (Prieto, Villagrá-Sobrino, et al., 2011). Learning scientists are designing new scripts that are flexible enough to adapt to different curricular goals and different teaching styles. When the script is open-ended enough to support classroom improvisations, teachers can use their professional judgement to improvise on the script as they continually balancing the teaching paradox.

FROM NOVICE TEACHER TO EXPERT IMPROVISER

It takes time to become comfortable with the teaching paradox, and many new teachers are understandably nervous about their ability to improvise.

In fact, beginners in nearly every profession—not just in teaching—like to have step-by-step instructions on how to do things efficiently. It's normal to ask for specifics on how to manage the classroom, how to organize their curriculum, how to develop assessments that align with local and national standards, how to manage group work, and how to fairly assign grades (Bransford, Derry, Berliner, Hammerness, & Beckett, 2005). Beginning teachers can find these specific instructions in their teaching methods textbooks. As I noted in Chapter 3, these textbooks focus almost exclusively on techniques that provide more structure to a class, and that's valuable to a beginning teacher. But as teachers gain confidence, as they master the more scripted techniques, they become comfortable with guided improvisation.

Research on teacher expertise has found that beginning teachers benefit from more scaffolding when they're first learning how to teach, just as students need more scaffolding at the beginning of a new unit. The teachers in Ana de Austria liked using the orchestration script; it helped them with the difficult challenge of revising their lesson plans and instructional strategies to take the best advantage of new technologies. As you learn and grow as a teacher, the scaffolds can be faded so that your classroom will become increasingly improvisational. The transition from novice to expert teacher is one of progressively less structure and more and more improvisation.

Many teacher careers tend to go through roughly three stages of expertise (Boote, 2004; Tsui, 2003):

1. In the first stage of a career, beginning teachers are learning how to develop and deliver a coherent curriculum, and their lesson plans are relatively structured.
2. After a few years, teachers enter a second stage of development. They now can look back on what happens in the classroom each day, reflect on their own actions, and adapt their plans for the next day.
3. In the third and final stage of expertise, teachers can go beyond the structures of existing curriculum options, and they're able to create their own new curricula and classroom practices.

The scaffolds provided by preservice methods textbooks are essential for beginning teachers. As you master the routines, they'll become comfortable and familiar. Think of these structures as training wheels. Continuously reflect on your own teaching practice and be aware of how your lesson plans balance structure and improvisation. Work toward fading these classroom scripts and developing your own ability to guide improvisation. Take off the training wheels and fly!

TEACHING IMPROV GAMES

Nicole Shechtman and Jennifer Knudsen (2011) created an intensive 2-week summer PD workshop for middle school teachers from high-poverty districts in the San Francisco Bay area, centered around a set of teaching improv games (TIGs). The goal was to help the teachers teach the deep and big math themes of proportional reasoning and coordinate geometry. For example, one game called Why, Why, Why? was focused on a concept central to proportionality but sometimes not deeply understood by teachers: a justification for why cross-multiplication works for evaluating the equivalence of fractions.

The goal of the workshop was to help teachers guide students to creative knowledge by scaffolding students in argumentation practices. Student participation in argumentation practices has been found to lead to creative knowledge in math, including conceptual understanding and adaptive reasoning.

The workshop taught "teaching moves" that research has shown help to facilitate student argumentation skills, like "encourage students to take ownership of a position" or "elicit agreement or disagreement." Their workshop was designed around TIGs that had three parts that corresponded to the structure of a good argument: conjecturing, justifying, and concluding.

When the researchers compared the amount of student mathematical argumentation in these teachers' classrooms to other teachers who didn't have the workshop, they found a lot more student argumentation—and it was effective argumentation for learning.[2]

IMPROVISING WITH PEDAGOGICAL CONTENT KNOWLEDGE

To teach with guided improvisation, you have to have a deep understanding of your subject. If all you've learned is shallow knowledge, then how could you teach creative knowledge?. You wouldn't be able to guide students through a learning trajectory to creative knowledge if you didn't know what creative knowledge looked like.

People say those who can't do, teach. They are so wrong! Even more wrong than most people realize. It's more accurate to say that experts who *can* do—for example, a professional research scientist, or nationally ranked chess player, or a world-class chef—usually *can't* teach what they know. To teach with guided improvisation, it's not enough to have subject-area content knowledge. You need *pedagogical content knowledge*, the ability to teach in ways that are specific and unique to your subject (Shulman, 1987). Here's what research shows that teachers need to be effective to teach with guided improvisation:

1. Teaching for creativity requires teachers to have *content knowledge*. They have to know almost as much as a professional in their field. You learn content knowledge in your subject-area courses.
2. Teaching for creativity requires teachers to have *pedagogical knowledge*. They have to know the techniques, skills, and tricks to manage and motivate students. You learn pedagogical knowledge in your teacher education courses.
3. But simply knowing the basic skills of how to teach doesn't prepare you to teach for creative knowledge. You need to be able to combine these two distinct types of knowledge in order to teach students with guided improvisation. Most graduates of teacher education programs, after a year or two on the job, say that they wished they'd learned more in their preservice program about how to combine content and pedagogical knowledge.

In instructionist classrooms—where the teacher develops a highly structured plan for the day, does most of the talking, and stays in control of the classroom—you can get by with a limited understanding of content and a few simple pedagogical techniques. You don't need the creative knowledge and adaptive expertise that supports you in guided improvisation (Feiman-Nemser & Buchmann, 1986; Shulman, 1987). But pedagogical content knowledge—the kind of knowledge that supports guided improvisation—is a type of creative knowledge. When teachers have creative knowledge in their subject, they're prepared to teach with guided improvisation.

Some educational reformers have tried to remove the need to improvise altogether. They advocate *direct instruction*, where the teacher is given a word-for-word script to use for each day's class session (Sawyer, 2011b). Direct instruction is sometimes called "teacher proofing" because almost anyone can do it. You don't need to know very much about teaching, and you definitely don't need creative knowledge or the ability to guide improvisational learning. If you're reading from a script, if the classroom is completely structured, you don't have to know much about the subject. Basically, you just have to be a good script reader—good at projecting your voice and holding the class's attention.

When teachers don't know a subject very well, they're more likely to structure their classes, and they're less likely to welcome creative responses and questions from students (Beghetto, 2009). But for creative learning outcomes, students should be encouraged to ask surprising questions without easy answers, as I showed in Chapter 2. The best teachers can improvise responses that guide students to think about their own questions in productive ways. To improvise a good response to an unexpected question, you'll often draw on subject-area knowledge that wasn't necessarily part of the lesson. Pedagogical content knowledge gives you the expertise you need to guide improvisation.

SUMMARY

The teaching paradox is ever-present and constantly changing. There's no formula that you can put in place at the beginning of the year in hopes that it will dispense with the paradox and allow you to forget about it for the rest of the year. In creative classrooms the balance of structure and improvisation is constantly changing, in every moment of every class. Even in the lesson charted in Figure 4.4, a highly structured class activity, students still retain some freedom to improvise their own learning within that structure. It's hard to predict when you'll need to introduce more structure, or when you should reduce structure and let students explore more freely.

Compared to teaching with instructionism, your first year of teaching with improvisation is going to be more challenging. The scripted nature of instructionism can give you confidence that you're doing what you're supposed to do. If you diverge from your lesson plan, at least you know what you did wrong, and you know how to fix it next time—just study the plan more, and make sure to stick with it.

Guided improvisation is hard. It takes a lot of confidence to stand in front of a class full of students, without knowing what the students might say or do; without knowing what knowledge or instructional strategy you'll need next to guide students forward; without knowing exactly what students will learn, or how long it might take them. You won't know how you'll respond until you do. It's frightening, at first. But as you gain experience, all the research shows that you'll learn how to improvise. You'll see that students are learning creative knowledge. They learn the required subject-area knowledge, but they learn a deeper conceptual understanding; an overall system and framework; an ability to think and explain with their knowledge; and an ability to adapt their knowledge, to transfer it to new situations, and to be creative with that knowledge. You'll see that students learn with greater retention and understanding.

As you see the benefits for students, year after year, you'll begin to trust in the power of guided improvisation to impact student learning. And you'll trust your own ability to guide each student to creative knowledge in your subject.

NOTES

1. For research on orchestration scripts, see Dillenbourg, Järvelä, and Fischer, 2009; Fischer and Dillenbourg, 2006; Prieto, Dlab, et al., 2011. Specific sources for the research study in Spain include Dimitriadis, 2012; and Prieto, Dlab, et al., 2011. These papers discuss a variety of concepts related to guided improvisation, including "recurrent routines": planned versus "enactment routines"; "formulaic improvisation"; and "paraphrase improvisation."

2. Sources for studies of argumentation skills and creative knowledge in math can be found in National Council of Teachers of Mathematics' Principles and Standards (2000–2004). Kilpatrick, Swafford, and Findell (2001) show that when students generate mathematical conjectures and justify their validity, they learn more creative knowledge in math, including conceptual understanding, procedural fluency, strategic competence, adaptive reasoning, and productive disposition.

CHAPTER 5

Schools for Creativity

Creativity is based on *creative knowledge*: a deep understanding of complex concepts, models, and frameworks (see Chapter 2). Creativity is a subject-specific ability, and creative education should focus on a new kind of teaching in each subject: guided improvisation that teaches creative knowledge in that subject (see Chapter 3). With guided improvisation, students learn subject-area knowledge better. They remember what they've learned, they understand it better, and they can apply what they've learned to a broad variety of problems. Most importantly, they can create with that knowledge.

In creative classrooms teachers guide students as they take an exploratory path through a learning trajectory that leads to creative knowledge. Students are guided by structured but adaptable lesson plans and classroom activities. The most effective creative teaching takes place in schools that are redesigned to support this new kind of pedagogy. In schools for creativity, everything is aligned with the creative mission: school culture, leadership, structure, and assessments. In this chapter, I describe how schools and teachers can work together to do the important work of teaching for creativity.

Schools are complex organizations, with many of the same challenges facing other organizations, both nonprofit and for-profit. Studies of innovative organizations have found that they share four important characteristics (Sawyer, 2017), and each of these applies to schools as well:

- A *culture* that values creative learning and knowing, instead of emphasizing coverage of shallow knowledge
- *Leaders* who prioritize creativity and give teachers the support they need
- An *organizational structure* that supports teaching for creativity
- *Assessments* that focus on creative knowledge as well as shallow knowledge

Throughout this book, I've described schools that are doing a great job at teaching for creativity. All of these schools share these same four characteristics. In the following four sections, I draw on this research to describe what creative schools look like—in their culture, leadership, structure, and assessment.

THE CULTURE OF THE CREATIVE SCHOOL

The *culture* of a school includes the hidden, unstated beliefs shared by everyone, and the social practices and ways of thinking and acting that everyone takes for granted. The beliefs and practices seem so normal that no one thinks to question them. They seem natural. It's just the way things are.

A school's culture makes it easier to teach in some ways, and harder to teach in other ways. In many schools these cultural beliefs and practices are silently and invisibly aligned with instructionism. In such schools it can be challenging to teach for creative knowledge.

For example, a common cultural assumption is that students should be quiet and listen to what the teacher is saying. Students need to memorize what she says. We know that this pedagogy doesn't work, but it's hard to change deep-seated cultural assumptions. Remember, in Chapter 1, when I described the sketches of teachers that children draw? They all drew a woman, standing in front of a blackboard, and lecturing to the class. When a parent visits an instructionist classroom, they see what they think a school is: They see kids sitting in rows, quiet and paying attention. They see the teacher standing at the front, talking about the day's scheduled unit in the textbook. What they see is reassuringly familiar because it aligns with the unstated cultural assumptions of instructionism.

Because these assumptions are so deeply embedded, transforming schools requires us to challenge these assumptions directly. Teachers can play an important role in changing a school's culture from instructionism to creativity. The first step in cultural change is to make explicit the community's unstated instructionist assumptions. Next, share the research, summarized in this book, showing that instructionism leads to knowledge that's not understood and that's forgotten immediately. Then you're ready to ask the school community the most important question: "What do we value? Is this what we want our students to learn?" In most schools the answer will be a firm and resounding "No." Now you're ready to work together to build a creative school.

I would suggest that you also spend some time helping students learn how to succeed in this new kind of classroom. When students first experience guided improvisation, they sometimes push back. They won't be able to use the classroom behaviors and strategies that worked for them in instructionist classrooms. Our views of how to be a good student are based on deep-rooted cultural assumptions. When a class first transitions to guided improvisation, some students may find that it's not as easy for them as instructionism. In fact, research confirms that learning for creative knowledge takes more effort than memorizing shallow knowledge (Brown et al., 2014). Many students are used to classes that are more structured, and when they're asked to improvise, they won't know what to do. Guided improvisation is ambiguous and unpredictable, and many students find this to be frustrating—in the same way that teachers experience anxiety when they first start teaching this way. And as I showed in Chapters 2 and 3, when students are learning with guided improvisation, they're going to encounter dead ends, they'll fail, and they'll take a lot more time than with instructionism. At first, they'll ask you to give them more structure and more detail, and to be more clear about exactly what you want them to do. It can be hard to say no, but it's important not to add too much structure to their creative explorations. Too much guidance prevents the students from engaging in creative, emergent learning (Kind & Kind, 2007).

I don't think it will take that long to convince students. In my own classes, I take the first week of the semester to describe the project-based pedagogy that I'll be using. I give the students a short handout with a summary of the research showing that instructionism is ineffective, and showing that guided improvisation works. I've discovered that they're willing to give it a try. After all, students are fed up with instructionism. Surveys of high school students show that they want teachers to stop lecturing from textbooks. They want to learn in classes that use discovery-based, problem-based, and inquiry-based curricula (Agarwal, 2001). If you're honest with students about what you're doing and why, they won't be hard to convince.

Parents will also ask questions about this new pedagogy. Many have seen only instructionist teaching. That's probably what they remember from their own years in school. When you look through the lens of instructionism, the creative classroom sometimes seems out of control. Kevin Brookhouser, a teacher at the York School, says that at first, newcomers think they're seeing "wishy-washy land" (Chapter 1). Parents might think that the classroom is poorly managed and that the teacher isn't using class time effectively.

But once schools complete the transition, parents become some of the biggest supporters. A great example is the TransformSC initiative. In South Carolina, a 2012 report raised the alarm: Their schoolchildren weren't learning. Educators took up the challenge. They joined together with politicians, business leaders, and parents, and created a new vision they called *TransformSC* (sccompetes.org/transformsc/). The schools needed a dramatic cultural change. Parents, students, business leaders, politicians, and even some teachers held deep-seated instructionist assumptions. Moryah Jackson, one of the early contributors to the TransformSC initiative, said, "It's difficult to change culture. Everybody knows what schools usually look like, so we have some very strong ties to our schools. When we

> A culture of innovation nurtures freedom to try new ideas and allows failure, receives necessary resources, provides training and development of necessary skills, uses collaboration, and has broad support.
>
> From the South Carolina Innovation Initiative Planning Document (2012, p. 11).

start talking about completely redesigning a building so it doesn't even look like a school anymore, we run into some issues in the community" (Robinson & Aronica, 2015, pp. 229–230). Some parents worried that guided improvisation wasn't rigorous enough.

Jackson, and others, were encouraged by several schools where cultural change happened quickly. One example is River Bluffs High School, in Lexington, South Carolina. It was custom-built for creative learning. There are no textbooks; students learn from exploration and project work. Because there aren't textbooks, the school hallways don't need rows of lockers. But somehow, we all expect a school hallway to be lined with lockers! Some people complain because it doesn't look like a school. Jackson heard one parent dismissively say, "It looks like a Starbucks." But once the school's performance numbers came in, parents became enthusiastic advocates. River Bluffs, and schools like it, were so successful that other schools started to sign up. As of 2019, there were 65 schools from 23 districts, and six entire districts, in the TransformSC network (Robinson & Aronica, 2015, pp. 227 passim; South Carolina Innovation Initiative Steering Team, 2012).

LEADERSHIP IN THE CREATIVE SCHOOL

Teachers play a key role in the transition to a creative school. But teachers can't do it alone. They need support from their school's principal, district leaders, and even from local and state politicians. Schools for creativity have leaders who support creative classrooms and who advocate for this new vision for schools. It's not unusual for business leaders and politicians to say that our kids need to learn 21st-century skills, that we need creative graduates for the jobs of today. But these businessmen and politicians usually don't know the research showing that this will require a new kind of classroom, a redesigned curriculum, and new assessments that focus on creative knowledge. Instead, they think that schools simply need to do a better job of instructionism. Sometimes they argue that schools should expand the amount of material they're covering, to demonstrate that students are learning even more than before. But with expanded coverage, students are only learning more shallow knowledge, and they're not making any progress toward creative learning. Ironically, many of these recent policy initiatives for "creativity" end up *reducing* student creativity, as I showed in Chapter 2. They force teachers to use far too much structure, they assess only shallow knowledge, and they prevent the kind of teaching that leads to creative knowledge.

In interviews with over 1,000 teachers, researcher Mary Kay Schrek asked them, "What blocks you from being more creative in the classroom?" The most common answers had to do with top-down structures that

---

CREATIVE SCHOOL LEADERS

Look for these actions from your school leaders:

- School leaders shout, "We are a creative school!" They say it frequently, loudly, and publicly.
- School leaders understand the difference between creative knowledge and shallow knowledge. They tirelessly advocate for creativity as a central learning outcome.
- School leaders give teachers professional development opportunities that focus on innovative teaching and learning.
- School leaders put systems in place that consistently recognize and reward creative teaching.
- School leaders understand what a creative classroom looks like. They're prepared to persuade parents and other stakeholders that guided improvisation is research-based and effective.
- School leaders welcome suggestions on how to make the school more conducive to creative teaching and learning.
- School leaders realize that teachers need to continually experiment in the class, and that this will lead teachers to occasionally make mistakes and to encounter dead ends. School leaders are supportive when this happens.
- School leaders model their dedication to creative thinking and acting in their own job, by experimenting, iterating, and welcoming a nonlinear path to innovation.

(Adapted from Schrek, 2009, p. 126)

---

constrained classroom improvisations (Schrek, 2009). One teacher said, "Our district's curriculum gives you a step-by-step set of instructions. You are NOT allowed to deviate from the goals or activities in the unit. We are given six days to complete each unit. Each day is laid out at 10-, 15-, 20-, and 30-minute intervals with specifics for each section. This really limits creativity!" (p. 13). Other teachers said that their schools require them to use specific textbooks, curricula, and lesson plans. Their schools forbid teachers from using supplemental materials that aren't officially approved. With all of these top-down constraints, teachers can't plan for improvisation (see Chapter 3) because they have to stick with the script they're given. When a school imposes a scripted pedagogy, teachers can't guide students in the improvisations that lead to creative knowledge.

In schools for creativity, leaders know that teachers need strong and consistent support. Especially at the beginning of the transformation, leaders need to work hard to advocate on behalf of teachers.

THE ORGANIZATIONAL STRUCTURE OF THE CREATIVE SCHOOL

Many of today's school structures are designed for instructionism. In schools for creativity, these structures look very different.

The Daily Schedule. In instructionist schools, every class period is the exact same length. The assumption is that learning is simply a matter of covering as many chunks of knowledge as possible. When you envision the learning process as linear and straightforward, then each day's class is simply one more step toward the goal of "coverage." In schools for creativity, the open-ended projects that lead to creative knowledge almost always take more time than a 50-minute class period. Project-based learning (PBL) works best in class sessions of 90 minutes or more. At High Tech High (HTH), a public charter school in San Diego, the entire curriculum is project-based. The school divides each day into longer blocks of time to support the sustained engagement that drives creative learning (Robinson & Aronica, 2015, pp. 128–129).

The School Subjects. In instructionist schools, students learn in classrooms and class periods that each focus on one subject. The assumption is that knowledge and learning can be compartmentalized and isolated (see Chapter 2). But the best creative ideas emerge from interdisciplinary connections. Creative knowledge includes conceptual frameworks that are often shared by two or more different fields. In schools for creativity the class schedule might not be organized into compartmentalized subjects. There might be fewer daily class periods, with each class combining content from multiple subjects—content that links together in a complex conceptual framework.

The Classroom. When you leave instructionism behind, there are no lectures. Colleges won't need lecture halls. Classrooms won't need rows of desks. That's why the most innovative school districts are building new schools with furniture that enables reconfigurable learning studio spaces that support project work. The top school furniture makers—Steelcase and Herman Miller—now employ education experts who have read a lot of the same research I've talked about in this book. They're already betting that schools will leave instructionism behind. They don't know how long it will be before this transformation happens, but they don't think it's very far off, and they want to be ready. They now sell chairs without desks attached (to make it easier for students to move actively and to collaborate in groups) and tables with wheels (so that students can form and reform groups). They sell "music stands" that are designed to display a tablet computer to a group (Nair, 2014).

San Diego's High Tech High, for example, doesn't have traditional classrooms. Instead, they've replaced desks and lecture podiums with a variety of creative learning spaces. These include *project studios*, where teams plan and construct models and prototypes; *construction labs* for video, biotech, animation, and engineering; *conference rooms* for meetings and presentations; and *private workstations* where 11th- and 12th-graders work on self-directed projects for several hours each day (Pearlman, 2002, 2004).

Changing culture and leadership is hard, but at least it doesn't require you to buy a lot of new stuff. In contrast, structural changes are expensive. Schools have invested a lot of money in the furniture they already have, and most don't have a budget for new furniture. Structural changes are also challenging for the administration and staff. The rigid schedule of the instructionist school day makes it easier to assign classrooms and teachers and to tell students where they should be through the day.

I recommend that you address culture and leadership change first, and save these structural changes for last. Once a new culture and leadership are in place, then it's easier to make the argument for structural change, and for the new resources and administrative procedures that this might require.

ASSESSMENT IN THE CREATIVE SCHOOL

Today's high-stakes tests don't work for creative knowledge. For example, multiple-choice questions are designed for shallow knowledge. Shallow knowledge comes in tiny chunks, and each chunk can be assessed with just one question. As demands for more coverage increase, it's easy to add one more question for each new chunk of knowledge that students have to learn. If your vision of school improvement is to increase coverage, then the tests don't have to change; they just become longer.

But tests of shallow knowledge don't reveal creative knowledge. As I described in Chapter 1, two-thirds of all students can't solve a problem that requires them to apply the Pythagorean theorem, even though many of them could make calculations using the formula in class. As far as the school bureaucracy was concerned, once students "covered" it in class, they'd "learned" the theorem. But students could only use their shallow knowledge to solve problems *exactly* like the ones they were trained on.

Schools for creativity need assessments, just as much as traditional schools. It's a misconception that all testing is opposed to creativity; it's *instructionist* tests that are opposed to creativity. Even in creative schools teachers and students need to know if what they're doing is working. Creativity researchers have worked hard to develop an assessment of domain-general creativity with only limited success (Kaufman, Plucker, & Baer, 2008; Sawyer, 2012). But schools don't have to wait for a general creativity test. As I argued in Chapter 2, we need to teach for creativity in every subject, and to assess student learning of creative knowledge, we need to change the way we assess subject-area knowledge.

CAN YOU SAVE THE EAGLES?

Professor John Bransford, a learning scientist at the University of Washington, compared the creative knowledge of 5th-graders with that of college students. He gave both groups a problem that they hadn't considered before: "Develop a statewide recovery plan to protect bald eagles." Bransford was pretty sure that neither the 5th graders nor the college students would get far, because they hadn't learned the factual knowledge they needed. As he expected, the college students came up with solutions that were just as ineffective as the 5th-graders'. It seemed that the college students hadn't learned anything in their zoology and biology classes.

But then Bransford gave a second test, one that assessed their ability to think creatively. All of the students were given a chance to ask questions that would give them the information they needed to develop an effective eagle recovery plan. The 5th graders asked simple questions about individual eagles, like "What do they like to eat? How big are they?" In contrast, the college students asked questions about complex ecological systems, like "What kinds of ecosystems support eagles?" and "Do other animals need to be recovered before we can recover eagles?" They even asked questions about relevant laws and political dynamics.

The college students had learned creative knowledge, a deeper understanding of how to think. This creative knowledge didn't show up on a test based on shallow knowledge. But Bransford's new assessments showed that they'd learned for creative understanding.

(Bransford et al., 2005, p. 71; Bransford & Schwartz, 1999)

To assess for creative knowledge, we can follow the principles found in two established and effective assessments that capture creative knowledge: the College Work Readiness Assessment and the Program for International Student Assessment.

The College Work Readiness Assessment (CWRA) measures creative knowledge by presenting students with an open-ended problem and then giving them 90 minutes to solve it. A typical problem asks students to explore how a community-based health clinic can meet a growing immigrant population, or how to manage the traffic congestion caused by population growth. St. Andrew's, an independent private school in Delaware, has been using CWRA for years to assess student progress and to provide feedback to teachers about how to better teach for creative knowledge. John Austin, the academic dean, says that CWRA rewards his teachers when they foster student creative learning. Shallow knowledge tests of students can't tell him what he wants to know: "Are we teaching our students to think intelligently and critically, to do more than follow, but to find new paths to go down?" (Silva, 2009, p. 632).

ASSESSING CREATIVE KNOWLEDGE

Like PISA and CWRA, there are several other tests that emphasize creative knowledge instead of shallow knowledge.

Portfolio assessment. At Napa's New Technology High School (NTHS), just like at High Tech High, students develop digital portfolios throughout their 4 years that are published on the school website. These portfolios display their project work, internship reflections, teacher evaluations, and comments from parents and peers. You can see examples of student portfolios at NTHS on their website (/www.newtechhigh.org/portfolio).

PowerSource. Developed at UCLA by the CRESST research group, this test measures complex thinking and judgement skills. It is aligned with California state math standards for middle school pre-algebra. The assessments are formatted as narrative themes or graphic novels. It's been tested in over 70 schools (Silva, 2009).

The International Baccalaureate (IB) Diploma Program is a 2-year course of study used in over 2,000 schools in 130 countries. IB teaches and assesses creative knowledge in each subject. It includes some multiple-choice test items, but it also contains open-ended problem challenges, questions that require data analysis, case studies, and essay questions (International Baccalaureate Organization, 2004).

The Program for International Student Assessment (PISA) was developed by the United States in collaboration with over 30 other countries. Each country uses a version translated into its own language, and the test is designed to be truly universal—none of the questions is specific to the culture or history of any one country. Every 3 years, PISA is administered to a sample of 15-year-old students in these countries; in 2015, over 70 countries participated. U.S. students scored right in the middle of the pack, just about at the average of the 72 countries (Ripley, 2013).

Some U.S. educators dismiss these findings, saying that PISA is just another shallow test that doesn't assess what we really want our students to learn. But in fact, PISA is designed to assess creative knowledge. From what I've seen of PISA, it does a better job of measuring creative knowledge than most tests. PISA assesses students' ability to solve problems and their ability to think critically with creative knowledge. When it gives a multiple-choice question, it then asks students to write a few sentences explaining their answer. Trained raters read and evaluate these explanations for understanding.

PISA and CWRA are well-known tests, and they do a good job of assessing creative knowledge. The biggest barrier to implementation is that they're expensive to use. When compared to instructionist tests, CWRA and PISA cost around 40 times as much per student! The multiple-choice tests that assess only for shallow knowledge cost less than one dollar per test (Government Accounting Office, 2003). The CWRA costs as much as $40 per student (Silva, 2009). And with PISA, it takes about an hour for a trained rater to score a single student's test (Ripley, 2013). Tests of creative knowledge will cost more to administer and score. I've never seen an effective test for creative knowledge that's multiple-choice, paper-and-pencil, and can be scored by computer.

When schools start to use tests like PISA and CWRA, the failures of instructionist pedagogy become obvious to everyone. Students who learn creative knowledge through guided improvisation do dramatically better on assessments of creative knowledge (Grossman, Schoenfeld, & Lee, 2005, p. 221). And they do just as well, sometimes better, on today's existing tests of shallow knowledge. This is really impressive once you realize that these students didn't "cover" all of the material they were being tested on, while the instructionism students had "covered" all of it. If a school uses only shallow-knowledge tests, you won't see that guided improvisation is better. If the test results are the same, leaders will ask, why make the effort to transform the culture or the schedule of the school day or the way we're running things? School leaders might conclude that it's just not worth the extra time and effort.

But convincing a school to spend 40 times as much on testing is a hard case to make, until you've shown that it works. To demonstrate the superiority of guided improvisation, you can start with a lower-cost approach. Select a small but representative sample of students and teach them with guided improvisation. Then test these students and compare their performance to the students who continued with instructionism. When you test for creative knowledge, the power of guided improvisation will be obvious to everyone.

ॐ

Keels Elementary School, in Columbia, South Carolina, has transformed itself into a creative school, and the students are thriving (Darling-Hammond et al., 2008, pp. 200–204). Keels shows what's possible with this new culture, leadership, structure, and assessment. Keels is near a military base, so quite a few of the students are new each year, as military families are transferred to and from the base. The majority of the local student body are students of color, and family incomes are far below average. The school was almost closed 20 years ago due to low scores. When you're threatened with closure, you have to change or die, and Keels chose to change. The transformation took 4 years, but it worked. The school showed dramatic increases in student test scores. It's not because they cherry-picked the best students: Half of the children who start Keels do not meet kindergarten readiness standards. But by the end of 1st grade, more than 90% do.

The leaders at Keels demonstrated a strong commitment to creative teaching and learning. The principal empowered teachers as expert professionals, and the teachers then knew that they had the support and commitment they needed. They worked together to design a new way of teaching, with changes that included the following:

- Cooperative learning in interdisciplinary classes
- Integrated instruction in reading and writing, and math and science
- A problem-based learning approach to social studies
- Computer-based learning units
- After-school programs for tutoring and supervised homework

The teachers developed new tests that assessed deep, adaptive, and creative knowledge, replacing tests for shallow knowledge. In science, for example, they started using performance assessments and portfolio assessments.

Keels Elementary has the culture, leadership, structure, and assessment associated with schools for creativity. Keels shows how we can redesign schools to support innovative teaching and learning.

SUMMARY

Creative schools, like River Bluffs High School and Keels Elementary School, look very different from traditional schools. They've transformed almost everything:

- They have a **culture** that encourages teacher creativity and fosters collaboration between teachers.
- They have **leaders** that give teachers autonomy and support them in teaching for creativity.
- They have a different **organizational structure**. Teacher and student work is organized to support flexible collaborations between teachers, even across different subjects, with a variety of classroom designs, and with daily schedules that support guided improvisation.
- **Assessment** is expanded and deepened so that creative knowledge in each subject is revealed and rewarded.

The examples throughout this book show that any school can teach for creativity—in any community and with all students. In these schools teachers are given the autonomy they need to develop flexible lesson plans and to improvisationally adapt them for each classroom. School leaders give them the flexibility to improvise a path through the unit that they think optimizes each student's learning trajectory.

But more than anything else—more than culture, leadership, structure, and assessment—schools need teachers who know how to guide classroom improvisation and who are committed to teaching for creative knowledge. In Chapter 6 I describe what you can do—together with other teachers—to build the creative school of the future.

A Call to Action

In creative classrooms students learn the subject-area knowledge they need—the same knowledge they would learn in a traditional classroom. But they learn that subject in a very different way: They learn *creative knowledge*. To be creative in a subject, you have to learn that subject in ways that prepare you to understand deeply, to adapt what you learn to new situations, and to build on past knowledge to innovate. Traditional classroom instruction is designed for *shallow knowledge*—facts and procedures that are fixed, authoritative, and unchanging. To be sure, students need to learn a lot of facts and procedures to master a subject. And you can't be creative in a subject if you haven't learned many important facts and procedures for each subject. After all, students don't need to re-create all human knowledge from scratch; creativity builds on what came before. But in the 21st century it's not enough for students to simply memorize knowledge from the past. We need to prepare our students to be creative with the knowledge they're learning.

For students to learn to be creative, we have to change almost everything about the way we teach. We can't just add more arts classes, while we keep teaching science and math the same traditional way. We can't just give students creativity training, if they keep learning only shallow knowledge in their subjects. Students simply can't be creative with shallow knowledge. Creativity requires a different kind of subject-area knowledge: Creative knowledge that includes deeper conceptual understanding, an ability to create and work with explanatory models, and connected networks of information. Creative knowledge is flexible and adaptable. Creative knowledge supports thinking in new ways, experimenting with new ideas and solutions, and building new knowledge.

I've shared stories about schools that are filled with innovative teaching and learning. I've described creative classrooms in public schools and private schools, in suburban schools and inner-city charters, with affluent populations and underserved students. I've shown the power of creative classrooms in every subject, including history, math, second language instruction, and science. In all of these examples, students learn their subjects more effectively than in traditional schools. Students in creative classrooms perform better on every test, and at the same time they learn in ways that

---

THE SEVEN HABITS OF HIGHLY CREATIVE TEACHERS

1. Creative teachers listen to students. They build on student actions to guide classroom improvisations.
2. Creative teachers are flexible thinkers. They're willing to change their plans in response to unexpected developments or new information.
3. Creative teachers are problem solvers. They can approach problems from new angles; they have techniques to deal with problems with incomplete information; they can work within ambiguity and confusion.
4. Creative teachers are empathetic. They can perceive a situation from another's point of view.
5. Creative teachers welcome humor. They create situations that are funny; they recognize funny ideas and situations; they can laugh at themselves.
6. Creative teachers are aware of how they're thinking and acting. They reflect on what works and how they can adapt their teaching next time.
7. Creative teachers view failures as learning opportunities.

(Schrek, 2009, pp. 102–103; drawing on Costa & Kallick, 2008, pp. 395–401)

---

prepare them to be creative. These examples show that we don't have to choose between creativity and state standards. Students learn everything better in creative classrooms.

I've drawn on the latest scientific studies to show that students learn creative knowledge most effectively through a pedagogy that I call *guided improvisation*. Guided improvisation is related to many research-based curricular innovations, including constructivism, group collaboration, project-based learning, design thinking, serious games, and exploratory maker activities. Guided improvisation builds on these successful innovations and gives teachers practical advice for how to design lesson plans and how to engage with students in the classroom. A lot of this advice is inspired by improvisational theater. In an improv performance, actors create their dialogue without a script. The flow of the performance unfolds in front of the audience. It's unpredictable; even the performers don't know what will happen next. The uncertainty can be terrifying! In fact, if there weren't any structure at all, a performance could wander aimlessly, and the audience would be confused or bored. That's why actors have developed a set of rules and open-ended plans that guide each performance. They improvise together, but these loose plans and rules guide their improvisation toward greater success. Stage actors and jazz musicians alike know that improvisation always takes place guided by loose and open-ended structures.

In creative classrooms students improvise together as they explore open-ended problems—inquiring and experimenting—and construct their own solutions. But these classroom improvisations aren't chaotic and aimless; the students are guided by scaffolds provided by the teacher. Students improvise their own path through a learning trajectory, but each student's path leads to a mastery of the required subject-area knowledge.

The research is convincing: Students learn better from guided improvisation. Instructionism is ineffective, especially at teaching the creative knowledge that students need in the 21st century. So why do we still find instructionism in so many schools? I think it's persistent because it's predictable and linear. It's easier for students. When you know what you're supposed to learn, you can walk down a linear, straightforward path to the answer. But learning scientists have found that effective learning takes a lot more effort than memorization. And for teachers, guided improvisation is more challenging than instructionism because "guidance" and "improvisation" are always in tension. In creative classrooms teachers are skilled professionals who manage this tension every day. They're ready to face the challenges of teaching for creativity. Creative teachers realize that guided improvisation results in better learning than scripted, linear lesson plans. Creative teachers know how to guide students as they develop creative solutions to open-ended problems. In creative classrooms students learn subject matter in ways that realize their creative potential.

In Chapter 1, I described the challenges that we face today: All too many schools are designed for an ineffective pedagogy that I call *instructionism*. In these traditional schools, students are given facts and procedures to memorize, and they're tested on their ability to remember. Instructionist classrooms are often structured and well-organized. The lesson plan stays on track, and students cover the material scheduled for each day. Everyone learns the same things, in the same sequence. It sounds reassuring and familiar; after all, that's the type of school most of us attended. But research repeatedly shows that instructionism is ineffective. Students don't understand what they're learning, they don't know why they're learning it, and they forget it right away. Students don't learn to be creative.

In Chapter 2, I defined *creativity* as a way of thinking that's grounded in *creative knowledge*: a deep understanding of complex concepts, models, and frameworks. To be creative in a subject, you need creative knowledge in that subject. Instructionism can never teach for creativity because it's designed for a superficial kind of knowledge that I call *shallow knowledge*. Shallow knowledge is fixed and rigid; it's isolated and compartmentalized. Creative knowledge is different from shallow knowledge in every way. It's deep rather than superficial; it's complex rather than simple; it's connected rather than compartmentalized; it's flexible rather than frozen and unchanging. Creative knowledge supports thinking and acting in new, unexpected situations. Creative knowledge prepares students for future learning.

Creative classrooms are the future of teaching and learning. In every subject the latest standards and assessments are based on creative knowledge. In science, the Next Generation Science Standards (NGSS) focus on creative knowledge—including the seven crosscutting concepts, such as *patterns* and *system models* (see Chapter 2). In math, the Common Core State Standards (CCSS) emphasize *mathematical thinking*—the ability to creatively solve new problems that haven't been encountered in the classroom. In history, students are now asked to learn broad, generally applicable concepts, including *change over time* (what causes change, and what forms does it take? How does each specific event contribute to patterns of change over time?) and *conflicting individual accounts* (how does a person's position in society influence how they perceive the same event? How can we explain and reconcile different accounts?). In creative classrooms students learn for 21st-century standards.

In Chapter 3, I described *guided improvisation*, a research-based pedagogy that teaches students creative knowledge. Students are presented with open-ended problems that don't have obvious solutions and don't have clear linear paths to the answer. Teachers give students the freedom to actively construct their own knowledge, as they improvise a nonlinear path to a solution. But students aren't given complete freedom. They're guided through a *learning trajectory* by the teacher. Teachers improvise together with the students throughout the class session, and they provide guidance that responds to each student. The uncertainty of improvisation can be stressful and challenging, especially when compared to the predictable, linear flow of an instructionist classroom. To help teachers learn to improvise, I described a variety of techniques that improv actors use. I showed how to adapt these techniques in your classroom to help you become more comfortable with guided improvisation.

In the creative classroom, structure and improvisation are always in tension. I call this tension the *teaching paradox* because it's unavoidable and because there's no single correct balance. The most effective balance keeps changing, depending on your curricular goals, your subject, your students, and where students are in their learning trajectory. In Chapter 4, I described guided improvisation in six different learning environments, including makerspaces, science centers, and project-based classrooms. Each of these six addresses the teaching paradox with a different balance of structure and improvisation. But in each case the balance is appropriate for the subject, the intended learning outcome, and the student's level of understanding.

In Chapter 5, I described schools where creative classrooms thrive. These schools have aligned everything to support innovative teaching and learning: culture, leadership, structure, and assessment. Traditional instructionist schools aren't designed this way, and many of them will need to go through a dramatic transformation. I give examples of schools that have successfully made the transition, and I describe the school cultures and organizational structures that support teachers in creative classrooms.

Teachers can play a key role in this transformation. But no teacher can do it alone. School change is a collaborative effort. When teachers come together with a shared commitment to creativity, they can build new school cultures and structures that support creative classrooms. At innovative schools like Keels Elementary (Chapter 5), teachers collaborate constantly, and they're more likely to watch each other teach. When teachers visit each other's classes, their teaching improves and their students learn better—as demonstrated by a 2015 study of 900 teachers in the Miami-Dade County Public Schools (MDCPS). The study found that at schools with more and better teacher collaboration, students learned more effectively. Student test scores were highest when teachers said that their collaboration was "extensive" and "helpful." Teachers improved more from year to year than in schools without a collaborative culture (Ronfeldt, Farmer, McQueen, & Grissom, 2015).

Teacher collaboration is a key to success in the world's best schools. In countries where students get the highest scores on international tests, teachers are more likely to watch each other teach (Ripley, 2013, p. 216). For example, the collaborative practice of *lesson study* is widely used in Japan, China, Australia, and New Zealand. In lesson study, teachers develop new lesson plans together. Then they watch while one person teaches the new lesson. Afterward they meet to reflect on what worked and how they could improve their new lesson design (Watanabe, 2002). When teachers work together, everyone's classroom becomes more effective at fostering creative learning. Teachers share instructional strategies and lesson plans that effectively balance the teaching paradox. Teachers experiment, and they don't hide it when they fail. They share what worked and what didn't. They collaborate with other teachers to build innovative 21st-century schools.

In a creative classroom, students understand what they're learning. They think creatively as they approach new problems, and they adapt their knowledge to new situations. They're prepared to go beyond what they've learned. In a creative classroom, students learn to be creative at the same time that they learn required subject-area knowledge. They're prepared to succeed on new assessments that emphasize creative knowledge. They're ready to make creative contributions that will change the world.

References

Abrahamson, D., & Lindgren, R. (2014). Embodiment and embodied cognition. In R. K. Sawyer (Ed.), *The Cambridge handbook of the learning sciences* (2nd ed., pp. 358–376). New York, NY: Cambridge.

Adams, J. L. (2001). *Conceptual blockbusting: A guide to better ideas* (4th ed.). New York, NY: Norton. (Original work published 1974 by the Stanford Alumni Association)

Agarwal, P. K. (2001, November). If I could make a school. *Learning and Leading with Technology, 29*(3), 28–31, 41.

Agarwal, P. K. (2019). Retrieval practice & Bloom's taxonomy: Do students need fact knowledge before higher order learning? *Journal of Educational Psychology, 111*(2), 189–209. Retrieved from eric.ed.gov/?id=EJ1205208

Allen, S. (1992). Student-sustained discussion: When students talk and the teacher listens. In N. A. Branscombe, D. Goswami, & J. Schwartz (Eds.), *Students teaching, teachers learning* (pp. 81–92). Portsmouth, NH: Boynton/Cook.

Anderson, L. W., & Krathwohl, D. R. (Eds.). (2001). *A taxonomy for learning, teaching, and assessing: A revision of Bloom's taxonomy of educational objectives.* New York: Addison Wesley Longman, Inc.

Azmitia, M. (1996). Peer interactive minds: Developmental, theoretical, and methodological issues. In P. B. Baltes & U. M. Staudinger (Eds.), *Interactive minds: Life-span perspectives on the social foundation of cognition* (pp. 133–162). New York, NY: Cambridge University Press.

Baer, J. (1996). The effects of task-specific divergent-thinking training. *Journal of Creative Behavior, 30*(3), 183–187.

Baker-Sennett, J., & Matusov, E. (1997). School "performance": Improvisational processes in development and education. In R. K. Sawyer (Ed.), *Creativity in performance* (pp. 197–212). Norwood, NJ: Ablex.

Barnes, D., & Rosen, H. (Eds.) (1969). *Language, the learner and the school.* Baltimore, MD: Penguin. (Revised edition, 1971).

Bearison, D. J., Magzamen, S., & Filardo, E. K. (1986). Socio-cognitive conflict and cognitive growth in young children. *Merrill-Palmer Quarterly, 32*(1), 51–72.

Beghetto, R. A. (2009). In search of the unexpected: Finding creativity in the micromoments of the classroom. *Psychology of Aesthetics, Creativity, and the Arts, 3*(1), 2–5.

Bell, D. (1973). *The coming of the post-industrial society: A venture in social forecasting.* New York, NY: Basic Books.

Belland, B. R., Walker, A. E., & Kim, N. J. (2017). A Bayesian network meta-analysis to synthesize the influence of contexts of scaffolding use on cognitive outcomes in STEM education. *Review of Educational Research, 87*(6), 1042–1081.

Berliner, D. C. (1987). Ways of thinking about students and classrooms by more and less experienced teachers. In J. Calderhead (Ed.), *Exploring teachers' thinking* (pp. 60–83). London, United Kingdom: Cassell Education Limited.

Berliner, D. C., & Tikunoff, W. J. (1976). The California beginning teacher study. *Journal of Teacher Education, 27*(1), 24–30.

Berliner, P. F. (1994). *Thinking in jazz: The infinite art of improvisation.* Chicago, IL: University of Chicago Press.

Bloom, B. S., Engelhart, M. D., Furst, E. J., Hill, W. H., & Krathwohl, D. R. (1956). *Taxonomy of educational objectives: The classification of educational goals. Handbook 1: Cognitive domain.* New York, NY: Longman, Green.

Boote, D. N. (2004, April). *Teachers' professional discretion and the curricula.* Paper presented at the annual meeting of the American Educational Research Association, San Diego, CA.

Borko, H., & Livingston, C. (1989). Cognition and improvisation: Differences in mathematics instruction by expert and novice teachers. *American Educational Research Journal, 26*(4), 473–498.

Bransford, J. D., Brown, A. L., & Cocking, R. R. (Eds.). (2000). *How people learn: Brain, mind, experience, and school.* Washington, DC: National Academies Press.

Bransford, J. D., Derry, S., Berliner, D., Hammerness, K., & Beckett, K. L. (2005). Theories of learning and their roles in teaching. In L. Darling-Hammond & J. D. Bransford (Eds.), *Preparing teachers for a changing world: What teachers should learn and be able to do* (pp. 40–87). San Francisco, CA: Jossey-Bass.

Bransford, J. D., & Schwartz, D. L. (1999). Rethinking transfer: A simple proposal with multiple implications. *Review of Research in Education, 24*, 61–100.

Brennan, K. (2012). *Best of both worlds: Issues of structure and agency in computational creation, in and out of school* (Doctoral dissertation, Massachusetts Institute of Technology, Cambridge, MA). Available from scholar.harvard.edu/kbrennan/publications/best-both-worlds-issues-structure-and-agency-computational-creation-and-out

Bronson, P., & Merryman, A. (2010, July 19). The creativity crisis. *Newsweek, 44–50.*

Brown, M., & Edelson, D. C. (2001, April). *Teaching by design: Curriculum design as a lens on instructional practice.* Paper presented at the annual meeting of the American Educational Research Association, Seattle, WA.

Brown, P. C., Roediger, H. L., & McDaniel, M. A. (2014). *Make it stick: The science of successful learning.* Cambridge, MA: The Belknap Press/Harvard University Press.

Carnegie Corporation of New York. (2009). *The opportunity equation: Transforming mathematics and science education for citizenship in the global economy.* New York, NY: Institute for Advanced Study: Commission on Mathematics and Science Education.

Carretero, M., & Lee, P. (2014). Learning historical concepts. In R. K. Sawyer (Ed.), *The Cambridge handbook of the learning sciences* (2nd ed., pp. 587–604). New York, NY: Cambridge University Press.

Cazden, C. B. (2001). *Classroom discourse: The language of teaching and learning* (2nd ed.). Portsmouth, NH: Heinemann.

Chen, C.-H., & Yang, Y.-C. (2019). Revisiting the effects of project-based learning on students' academic achievement: A meta-analysis investigating moderators. *Educational Research Review, 26* (pp. 71-81).

Cobb, P. (1995). Mathematical learning and small-group interaction: Four case studies. In P. Cobb & H. Bauersfeld (Eds.), *The emergence of mathematical meaning: Interaction in classroom cultures* (pp. 25–129). Hillsdale, NJ: Erlbaum.

Cochrane-Smith, M., & Lytle, S. L. (1999). The teacher research movement: A decade later. *Educational Researcher, 28*(7), 15–25.

Cole, K. C. (2009). *Something incredibly wonderful happens: Frank Oppenheimer and the world he made up.* New York, NY: Houghton Mifflin Harcourt.

Confrey, J. (2006). The evolution of design studies as a methodology. In R. K. Sawyer (Ed.), *The Cambridge handbook of the learning sciences* (1st ed., pp. 135–151). New York, NY: Cambridge University Press.

Cooper, M. M., Caballero, M. D., Ebert-May, D., Fata-Hartley, C. L., Jardeleza, S. E., Krajcik, J. S., . . . Underwood, S. M. (2015). Challenge faculty to transform STEM learning. *Science Magazine, 350*(6258), 281–282.

Costa, A. L., & Kallick, B. (Eds.). (2008). *Learning and leading with habits of mind: 16 essential characteristics for success.* Alexandria, VA: Association for Supervision and Curriculum Development.

Craft, A. (2005). *Creativity in schools: Tensions and dilemmas.* New York, NY: Routledge.

Creason, D. (2017). *Creativity for Schools: Interview with Kevin Brookhouser.* Unpublished student research, School of Education. University of North Carolina, Chapel Hill, NC.

Cropley, A. J. (1997). Fostering creativity in the classroom: General principles. In M. A. Runco (Ed.), *Creativity research handbook* (Vol. 1, pp. 83–114). Cresskill, NJ: Hampton Press.

Dahn, M., Enyedy, N., & Danish, J. (2018, June). *How teachers use instructional improvisation to organize science discourse and learning in a mixed reality environment.* Paper presented at the 13th International Conference on the Learning Sciences (ICLS), London, United Kingdom.

Darling-Hammond, L. (1997). *The right to learn: A blueprint for creating schools that work.* San Francisco, CA: Jossey-Bass.

Darling-Hammond, L., Barron, B., Pearson, P. D., Schoenfeld, A. H., Stage, E. K., Zimmerman, T. D., . . . Tilson, J. L. (2008). *Powerful learning: What we know about teaching for understanding.* San Francisco, CA: Jossey-Bass.

Daro, P., Mosher, F. A., & Corcoran, T. (2011). *Learning trajectories in mathematics: A foundation for standards, curriculum, assessment, and instruction.* Philadelphia, PA: Consortium for Policy Research in Education.

Davidson, C. H. (2017, October 27). A newer education for our era. *The Chronicle of Higher Education,* B30–B31.

Davis, E. A., & Miyake, N. (Eds.). (2004). Scaffolding [Special issue]. *The Journal of the Learning Sciences, 13*(3).

Davis, M. (2017). *Teaching design: A guide to curriculum and pedagogy for college design faculty and teachers who use design in their classrooms.* New York, NY: Allworth Press.

DeZutter, S. (2008). *Cultural models of teaching in two non-school educational communities* (Unpublished doctoral dissertation). Washington University, St. Louis, MO.

DeZutter, S. (2011). Professional improvisation and teacher education: Opening the conversation. In R. K. Sawyer (Ed.), *Structure and improvisation in creative teaching* (pp. 27–50). New York, NY: Cambridge University Press.

Dillenbourg, P., Järvelä, S., & Fischer, F. (2009). The evolution of research in computer-supported collaborative learning: From design to orchestration. In N. Balacheff, S. Ludvigsen, T. de-Jong, A. Lazonder, & S. Barnes (Eds.), *Technology-enhanced learning: Principles and products* (pp. 3–19). Amsterdam, The Netherlands: Springer.

Dimitriadis, Y. A. (2012). Supporting teachers in orchestrating CSCL classrooms. In A. Jimoyiannis (Ed.), *Research on e-learning and ICT in education* (pp. 71–82). New York, NY: Springer.

Doise, W., & Mugny, G. (1984). *The social development of the intellect.* New York, NY: Pergamon Press.

Donaldson, J. (2018, April). *Public education and public perceptions of learning.* Paper presented at the annual meeting of the American Educational Research Association, New York, NY.

Drucker, P. F. (1994). The age of social transformation. *The Atlantic Monthly, 274,* 53–80.

EdVenture. (2017). *2017–2018 School Program Guide.* Retrieved from link to Field Trip Guide at www.edventure.org/columbia/educators/field-trips

Erickson, F. (1982). Classroom discourse as improvisation: Relationships between academic task structure and social participation structure in lessons. In L. C. Wilkinson (Ed.), *Communicating in the classroom* (pp. 153–181). New York, NY: Academic Press.

Exploratorium. (n.d.). Field trip chaperone guide: Energy on the move. Retrieved from www.exploratorium.edu/files/pdfs/Energy_on_the_Move-FT_Chaperone_Guide.pdf

Feiman-Nemser, S., & Buchmann, M. (1986). The first year of teacher preparation: Transition to pedagogical thinking? *Journal of Curriculum Studies, 18,* 239–256.

Feldhusen, J. F., & Treffinger, D. J. (1980). *Creative thinking and problem solving in gifted education.* Dubuque, IA: Kendall/Hunt.

Fischer, F., & Dillenbourg, P. (2006, April). *Challenges in orchestrating computer-supported collaborative learning.* Paper presented at the annual meeting of the American Educational Research Association, San Francisco, CA.

Fleith, D. d. S. (2000). Teacher and student perceptions of creativity in the classroom environment. *Roeper Review, 22*(3), 148–157.

Florida, R. (2002). *The rise of the creative class and how it's transforming work, life, community, and everyday life.* New York, NY: Basic Books.

Forman, E. A., & Cazden, C. B. (1985). Exploring Vygotskian perspectives in education: The cognitive value of peer interaction. In J. V. Wertsch (Ed.), *Culture, communication, and cognition: Vygotskian perspectives* (pp. 323–347). New York, NY: Cambridge University Press.

Friedman, T. L. (2005). *The world is flat: A brief history of the twenty-first century.* New York, NY: Farrar, Straus, & Giroux.

Gershon, W. (2006). Collective improvisation: A theoretical lens for classroom observation. *Journal of Curriculum and Pedagogy, 3*(1), 104–135.

Getzels, J. W., & Csikszentmihalyi, M. (1976). *The creative vision: A longitudinal study of problem finding in art.* New York: Wiley.

Gobet, F., Lane, P. C. R., Croker, S., Cheng, P. C.-H., Jones, G., Oliver, I., & Pine, J. M. (2001). Chunking mechanisms in human learning. *Trends in Cognitive Science, 5*(6), 236-243.

Government Accounting Office (GAO). (2003). *Title I: Characteristics of tests will influence expenses: Information sharing may help states realize efficiencies.* Washington, DC: Author.

Grossman, P., Schoenfeld, A., & Lee, C. (2005). Teaching subject matter. In L. Darling-Hammond & J. D. Bransford (Eds.), *Preparing teachers for a changing world* (pp. 201-231). San Francisco, CA: Jossey-Bass.

Halmos, P. R. (1968). Mathematics as a creative art. *American Scientist, 56*(4), 375–389.

Halverson, E. R., & Sheridan, K. M. (2014). The maker movement in education. *Harvard Educational Review, 84*(4), 495–504.

Hetland, L., & Winner, E. (2004). Cognitive transfer from arts education to non-arts outcomes: Research evidence and policy implications. In E. W. Eisner & M. D. Day (Eds.), *Handbook of research and policy in art education* (pp. 135–162). Mahwah, NJ: Erlbaum.

Hicks, D. (1995). Discourse, learning, and teaching. *Review of Research in Education, 21*, 49–95.

Housner, L. D., & Griffey, D. C. (1985). Teacher cognition: Differences in planning and interactive decision making between experienced and inexperienced teachers. *Research Quarterly for Exercise and Sport, 56*(1), 45–53.

Ingersoll, R. M. (2003). *Who controls teachers' work? Power and accountability in America's schools.* Cambridge, MA: Harvard University Press.

International Baccalaureate Organization. (2004). *Diploma programme assessment principles and practice.* Cardiff, Wales, United Kingdom: Author.

Israel, M., Maynard, K., & Williamson, P. (2013). Promoting literacy-embedded, authentic STEM instruction for students with disabilities and other struggling learners. *Teaching Exceptional Children, 45*, 18–25.

Järvelä, S., & Renninger, K. A. (2014). Designing for learning: Interest, motivation, and engagement. In R. K. Sawyer (Ed.), *The Cambridge handbook of the learning sciences* (2nd ed., pp. 668–685). New York, NY: Cambridge University Press.

Jonassen, D. H. (2000). Towards a design theory of problem solving. *Educational Technology, Research, and Development, 48*(4), 63–85.

Kapur, M. (2008). Productive failure. *Curriculum and Instruction, 26*(3), 379–424.

Kaufman, J. C. (2002). Narrative and paradigmatic thinking styles in creative writing and journalism students. *Journal of Creative Behavior, 36*(3), 201–219.

Kaufman, J. C., Plucker, J. A., & Baer, J. (2008). *Essentials of creativity assessment.* New York, NY: Wiley.

Kilpatrick, J., Swafford, J., & Findell, B. (2001). *Adding it up: Helping children learn mathematics.* Washington, DC: National Academies Press.

Kind, P. M., & Kind, V. (2007). Creativity in science education: Perspectives and challenges for developing school science. *Studies in Science Education, 43*, 1–37.

King, P., & Kitchener, K. (1994). *Developing reflective judgment: Understanding and promoting intellectual growth and critical thinking in adolescents and adults.* San Francisco, CA: Jossey-Bass.

Knudsen, J., & Shechtman, N. (2017). Professional development that bridges the gap between workshop and classroom through disciplined improvisation. In S. Goldman & Z. Kabayadondo (Eds.), *Taking design thinking to school* (pp. 163–179). New York, NY: Routledge.

Krajcik, J. S., & Shin, N. (2014). Project-based learning. In R. K. Sawyer (Ed.), *Cambridge Handbook of the Learning Sciences* (2nd ed., pp. 275–297). New York, NY: Cambridge University Press.

Krathwohl, D. R. (1994). Reflections on the taxonomy: Its past, present, and future. In L. W. Anderson & L. A. Sosniak (Eds.), *Bloom's taxonomy: A forty-year retrospective. Ninety-third yearbook of the National Society for the Study of Education. Part II* (pp. 181–202). Chicago, IL: University of Chicago Press.

Kuhn, D. (2015). Thinking together and alone. *Educational Researcher, 44*(1), 46–53.

Lamb, D. H. (2003). *Project based learning in an applied construction curriculum* (Master's thesis). Retrieved from California State University, San Bernardino, Theses Digitization Project (No. 2188), at scholarworks.lib.csusb.edu/etd-project/2188

Lampert, M., Rittenhouse, P., & Crumbaugh, C. (1996). Agreeing to disagree: Developing sociable mathematical discourse. In D. R. Olson & N. Torrance (Eds.), *The handbook of education and human development: New models of learning, teaching, and schooling* (pp. 731–764). Cambridge, MA: Blackwell.

Lehrer, R., & Schauble, L. (2006). Cultivating model-based reasoning in science education. In R. K. Sawyer (Ed.), *The Cambridge handbook of the learning sciences* (pp. 371–387). New York, NY: Cambridge University Press.

Leinhardt, G., & Greeno, J. G. (1986). The cognitive skill of teaching. *Journal of Educational Psychology, 78*(2), 75–95.

Lobman, C. (2011). Improvising within the system: Creating new teacher performances in inner-city schools. In R. K. Sawyer (Ed.), *Structure and improvisation in creative teaching* (pp. 73–93). New York, NY: Cambridge University Press.

Lobman, C., & Lundquist, M. (2007). *Unscripted learning: Using improv activities across the K–8 curriculum.* New York, NY: Teachers College Press.

Mack, R. W. (1987). Are methods of enhancing creativity being taught in teacher education programs as perceived by teacher educators and student teachers? *Journal of Creative Behavior, 21*, 22–33.

Mayer, R. E. (2010). *Applying the science of learning.* Upper Saddle River, NJ: Pearson.

Mayer, R. E., & Alexander, P. A. (Eds.). (2011). *Handbook of research on learning and instruction.* New York, NY: Routledge.

McCain, T., Jukes, I., & Crockett, L (2010). *Living on the future edge: Windows on tomorrow.* Thousand Oaks, CA: Corwin.

Mehan, H. (1979). *Learning lessons.* Cambridge, MA: Harvard.

Moore, M. T. (1985). The relationship between the originality of essays and variables in the problem-discovery process: A study of creative and non-creative middle school students. *Research in the Teaching of English, 19*(1), 84–95.

Nair, P. (2014). *Blueprint for tomorrow: Redesigning schools for student-centered learning.* Cambridge, MA: Harvard Education Press.

National Academy of Engineering. (2013). *Educating engineers: Preparing 21st century leaders in the context of new modes of learning: Summary of a forum.* Washington, DC: National Academies Press.

National Council of Teachers of Mathematics. (2000–2004). *Principles and standards for school mathematics: An overview.* Reston, VA: NCTM.

National Research Council. (1996). *National science education standards.* Washington, DC: National Academies Press.

National Research Council. (2011). *Successful K–12 STEM Education: Identifying effective approaches in science, technology, engineering, and mathematics.* Washington, DC: The National Academies Press.

National Research Council. (2012). *A framework for K–12 science education: Practices, crosscutting concepts, and core ideas.* Washington, DC: National Academies Press.

National Research Council. (2014). *Developing assessments for the Next Generation Science Standards.* Washington, DC: National Academies Press.

National Science Foundation (NSF). National Center for Science and Engineering

Statistics (NCSES). (2013). *Women, minorities, and persons with disabilities in science and engineering: 2013* (Special Report NSF 13-304). Arlington, VA: National Science Foundation.

NGSS Lead States. (2013). *Next generation science standards: For states, by states: Vol. 1. The standards.* Washington, DC: National Academies Press.

Nilssen, V., Gudmundsdottir, S., & Wangsmo-Cappelen, V. (1995, April). *Unexpected answers: A case study of a student teacher derailing in a math lesson.* Paper presented at the annual meeting of the American Educational Research Association, San Francisco, CA. Retreived from eric.ed.gov/?id=ED390853

OECD. (2008). *Innovating to learn, learning to innovate.* Paris, France: Author.

Olson, D. R. (2003). *Psychological theory and educational reform.* New York: Cambridge University Press.

Owens, T. (1974). *Charlie Parker: Techniques of improvisation* (Unpublished doctoral dissertation). University of California, Los Angeles, CA.

Pai, H., Sears, D. A., & Maeda, Y. (2015). Effects of small-group learning on transfer: A meta-analysis. *Educational Psychology Review, 27*(1), 79–102.

Paley, V. G. (1981). *Wally's stories.* Cambridge: Harvard University Press.

Palincsar, A. S. (1998). Social constructivist perspectives on teaching and learning. In J. T. Spence, J. M. Darley, & D. J. Foss (Eds.), *Annual Review of Psychology* (Vol. 49, pp. 345–375). Palo Alto, CA: Annual Reviews.

Partnership for 21st Century Skills. (2019). Framework for 21st century learning. Retrieved from static.battelleforkids.org/documents/p21/P21_Framework_Brief.pdf

Patrick, H., & Pintrich, P. R. (2001). Conceptual change in teachers' intuitive conceptions of learning, motivation, and instruction: The role of motivational and epistemological beliefs. In B. Torff & R. Sternberg (Eds.), *Understanding and teaching the intuitive mind: Student and teacher learning* (pp. 117–143). Mahwah, NJ: Erlbaum.

Pearlman, B. (2002). Designing, and making, the new American high school. *Technos Quarterly, 11*(1), 12–19. Retrieved from web.archive.org/web/20080720110319/, www.ait.net/technos/tq_11/1pearlman.php

Pearlman, B. (2004). Technology at High Tech High. Retrieved from www.bobpearlman.org/BestPractices/TechnologyatHighTechHigh.pdf

Pellegrino, J. W., & Hilton, M. L. (2012). *Education for life and work: Developing transferable knowledge and skills in the 21st century.* Washington, DC: National Academies Press.

Perret-Clermont, A. N. (1980). *Social interaction and cognitive development in children.* New York, NY: Academic Press.

Petrosino, A. J. (1998). *The use of reflection and revision in hands-on experimental activities by at-risk children* (Unpublished doctoral dissertation). Vanderbilt University, Nashville, TN.

Pfaffman, J. A. (2003). *Manipulating and measuring student engagement in computer-based instruction* (Unpublished doctoral dissertation). Vanderbilt University, Nashville, TN.

Phelps, E., & Damon, W. (1989). Problem solving with equals: Peer collaboration as a context for learning mathematics and spatial concepts. *Journal of Educational Psychology, 81*, 639-646.

Piirto, J. (2004). *Understanding creativity.* Scottsdale, AZ: Great Potential Press.

Pink, D. H. (2005). *A whole new mind: Why right-brainers will rule the future.* New York, NY: Riverhead Books.

President's Council of Advisors on Science and Technology (PCAST). (2012). Engage to excel: Producing one million additional college graduates with degrees in science, technology, engineering, and mathematics. Washington, DC: Executive Office of the President. Retrieved from files.eric.ed.gov/fulltext/ED541511.pdf

Prieto, L. P., Dlab, M. H., Gutiérrez, I., Abdulwahed, M., & Balid, W. (2011). Orchestrating technology-enhanced learning: A literature review and a conceptual framework. *International Journal of Technology Enhanced Learning, 3*(6), 583–598.

Prieto, L. P., Villagrá-Sobrino, S., Jorrín-Abellán, I. M., Martínez-Monés, A., & Dimitriadis, Y. (2011). Recurrent routines: Analyzing and supporting orchestration in technology-enhanced primary classrooms. *Computers & Education, 57*, 1214–1227.

Reiser, B. J., & Tabak, I. (2014). Scaffolding. In R. K. Sawyer (Ed.), *The Cambridge handbook of the learning sciences* (2nd ed., pp. 44–62). New York, NY: Cambridge University Press.

Rejskind, G. (2000). TAG teachers: Only the creative need apply. *Roeper Review, 22*(3), 153–157.

Richardson, V. (1996). The role of attitudes and beliefs in learning to teach. In J. Sikula, T. J. Buttery, & E. Guyton (Eds.), *Handbook of research on teacher education* (2nd ed., pp. 102–119). New York, NY: MacMillan.

Ripley, A. (2013). *The smartest kids in the world and how they got that way.* New York, NY: Simon & Schuster.

Robinson, K., & Aronica, L. (2015). *Creative schools: The grassroots revolution that's transforming education.* New York, NY: Penguin.

Rogoff, B. (1998). Cognition as a collaborative process. In D. Kuhn & R. S. Siegler (Eds.), *Handbook of child psychology: Vol. 2. Cognition, perception, and language* (5th ed., pp. 679–744). New York, NY: Wiley.

Ronfeldt, M., Farmer, S. O., McQueen, K., & Grissom, J. A. (2015). Teacher collaboration in instructional teams and student achievement. *American Educational Research Journal, 52*(3), 475–514.

Sahlberg, P. (2011). *Finnish lessons: What can the world learn from educational change in Finland?* New York, NY: Teachers College Press.

Sassi, A. M., & Goldsmith, L. T. (1995, October). *Beyond recipes and behind the magic: Mathematics teaching as improvisation.* Paper presented at the annual meeting of the North American Chapter of the International Group for the Psychology of Mathematics Education (PME-NA), Columbus, OH. Retrieved from eric.ed.gov/?id=ED389614

Sassi, A. M., Morse, A., & Goldsmith, L. T. (1997, March). *What makes for a good beginning? Improvising in an elementary mathematics teacher inquiry group.* Paper presented at the annual meeting of the American Educational Research Association, Chicago, IL.

Sawyer, R. K. (2003). *Improvised dialogues: Emergence and creativity in conversation.* Westport, CT: Ablex/Greenwood.

Sawyer, R. K. (2004a). Creative teaching: Collaborative discussion as disciplined improvisation. *Educational Researcher, 33*(2), 12–20.

Sawyer, R. K. (2004b). Improvised lessons: Collaborative discussion in the constructivist classroom. *Teaching Education, 15*(2), 189–201.

Sawyer, R. K. (Ed.) (2011a). *Structure and improvisation in creative teaching.* Cambridge, United Kingdom: Cambridge University Press.

Sawyer, R. K. (2011b). What makes good teachers great? The artful balance of structure and improvisation. In R. K. Sawyer (Ed.), *Structure and improvisation in creative teaching* (pp. 1–24). New York, NY: Cambridge University Press.

Sawyer, R. K. (2012). *Explaining creativity: The science of human innovation* (2nd ed.). New York, NY: Oxford University Press.

Sawyer, R. K. (2013). *Zig zag: The surprising path to greater creativity.* San Francisco, CA: Jossey-Bass.

Sawyer, R. K. (Ed.). (2014). *The Cambridge handbook of the learning sciences* (2nd ed.). New York, NY: Cambridge University Press.

Sawyer, R. K. (2015). A call to action: The challenges of creative teaching and learning. *Teachers College Record, 117*(10), 1–34.

Sawyer, R. K. (2017). *Group genius: The creative power of collaboration* (2nd ed.). New York, NY: BasicBooks.

Sawyer, R. K. (2018a). The role of failure in learning how to create. *Thinking Skills and Creativity.* Retrieved from doi.org/10.1016/j.tsc.2018.08.002

Sawyer, R. K. (2018b). Teaching and learning how to create in schools of art and design. *Journal of the Learning Sciences, 27*(1), 137–181.

Schacter, J., Thum, Y. M., & Zifkin, D. (2006). How much does creative teaching enhance elementary students' achievement? *Journal of Creative Behavior, 40*(1), 47–72.

Schmidt, W. A., & McKnight, C. C. (1997). *A splintered vision: An investigation of U.S. science and mathematics education.* Dordrecht, The Netherlands: Kluwer Academic.

Schrek, M. K. (2009). *Transformers: Creative teachers for the 21st century.* Thousand Oaks, CA: Corwin.

Schwartz, D. L., Bransford, J. D., & Sears, D. A. (2006). Efficiency and innovation in transfer. In J. P. Mestre (Ed.), *Transfer of learning from a modern multidisciplinary perspective* (pp. 1–51). Greenwich, CT: Information Age.

Schwartz, D. L., & Martin, T. (2004). Inventing to prepare for future learning: The hidden efficacy of encouraging original student production in statistics instruction. *Cognition and Instruction, 22*(2), 129–184.

Schwartz, D. L., Tsang, J. M., & Blair, K. P. (2016). *The ABCs of how we learn: 26 scientifically proven approaches, how they work, and when to use them.* New York, NY: Norton.

Scott, G., Leritz, L. E., & Mumford, M. D. (2004). The effectiveness of creativity training: A quantitative review. *Creativity Research Journal, 16*(4), 361–388.

The Secretary's Commission on Achieving Necessary Skills (SCANS). (1991). *What work requires of schools: A SCANS report for America 2000.* Washington, DC: U.S. Department of Labor. Retrieved from eric.ed.gov/?id=ED332054

Serrell, B. (1996). *Exhibit labels: An interpretive approach.* Walnut Creek, CA: Alta Mira Press.

Shechtman, N., & Knudsen, J. (2011). Bringing out the playful side of mathematics: Using methods from improvisational theater in professional development for urban middle school math teachers. In C. Lobman & B. E. O'Neill (Eds.), *Play and performance: Play & culture studies, Vol. 11* (pp. 94–116). Lanham, MD: University Press of America.

Shulman, L. S. (1987). Knowledge and teaching: Foundations of the new reform. *Harvard Educational Review, 57*(1), 1–22.

Shulman, L. S. (1999). Taking learning seriously. *Change, 31*(4), 10–17.

Silva, E. (2009). Measuring skills for 21st-century learning. *Phi Delta Kappan, 90*(9), 630–634.

Simon, M. A. (1995). Reconstructing mathematics pedagogy from a constructivist perspective. *Journal for Research in Mathematics Education, 26*(2), 114–145.

Singapore Ministry of Education. (2005). *Engaging our learners: Teach less, learn more.* Retrieved from eresources.nlb.gov.sg/printheritage/detail/dbe9f1f3-efcb-4bce-917b-1040e95ea179.aspx

Singapore Ministry of Education. (2015). *Nurturing students.* Retrieved from www.moe.gov.sg/education/education-system/nurturing-students

Smith, R. A. (1979). Is teaching really a performing art? *Contemporary Education, 51*(1), 31–35.

South Carolina Innovation Initiative Steering Team. (2012). *Report and recommendations.* Retrieved from sccompetes.org/project/innovation-initiative-steering-committee-report-and-recommendations/

Spear, K. (Ed.) (1984). Editor's notes. In K. Spear (Ed.), *Rejuvenating introductory courses* (pp. 1–9). San Francisco, CA: Jossey-Bass.

Spiro, R. J., Feltovich, P. J., Jacobson, M. J., & Coulson, R. L. (1991). Cognitive flexibility, constructivism, and hypertext: Random access instruction for advanced knowledge acquisition in ill-structured domains. *Educational Technology, 31*(5), 24–33.

Stahl, G., Koschmann, T., & Suthers, D. D. (2014). Computer-supported collaborative learning. In R. K. Sawyer (Ed.), *The Cambridge handbook of the learning sciences* (2nd ed., pp. 479–500). New York, NY: Cambridge University Press.

Sternberg, R. J., & Williams, W. M. (1996). *How to develop student creativity.* Alexandria, VA: Association for Supervision and Curriculum Development.

Stevens, R., Ramey, K., Meyerhoff, P., Hilppö, J., Kumpulainen, K., Kajamaa, A., . . . Halverson, R. (2018, June). *Exploring the adoption, spread, and sustainability of an informal STEAM learning innovation in schools.* Paper presented at the 13th International Conference of the Learning Sciences (ICLS), London, United Kingdom.

Stigler, J. W., Gonzales, P., Kawanaka, T., Knoll, S., & Serrano, A. (1999). *The TIMSS videotape classroom study* (NCES 99-074). Washington, DC: U.S. Department of Education, Office of Educational Research and Improvement. Retrieved from nces.ed.gov/pubs99/1999074.pdf

Tan, K., Tan, C., & Chua, J. (2008). Innovation in education: The "Teach Less, Learn More" initiative in Singapore schools. In J. E. Larkley & V. B. Maynhard (Eds.), *Innovation in education* (pp. 153–171). Hauppage, NY: Nova Science.

Thomas, J. W. (2000). *A review of research on project based learning.* Novato, CA: Buck Institute for Education.

Torrance, E. P. (1965). *Rewarding creative behavior: Experiments in classroom creativity.* Englewood Cliffs, NJ: Prentice-Hall.

Torrance, E. P. (1970). *Encouraging creativity in the classroom.* Dubuque, IA: W. C. Brown.

Trilling, B., & Fadel, C. (2009). *21st century skills: Learning for life in our times.* San Francisco, CA: Jossey-Bass.

Tsui, A.B.M. (2003). *Understanding expertise in teaching: Case studies of second language teachers.* New York, NY: Cambridge University Press.

Tudge, J., & Rogoff, B. (1989). Peer influences on cognitive development: Piagetian and Vygotskian perspectives. In M. Bornstein & J. Bruner (Eds.), *Interaction in cognitive development* (pp. 17–40). Hillsdale, NJ: Erlbaum.

Varian, H., & Lyman, P. (2003). *How much information?* Retrieved from groups.ischool.berkeley.edu/archive/how-much-info-2003/

Verba, M. (1994). The beginnings of collaboration in peer interaction. *Human Development, 37,* 125–139.

Vogel, G. (1996). Global review faults U.S. curricula. *Science, 274*(5286), 335.

Voss, J. F., & Carretero, M. (Eds.). (1998). *Learning and reasoning in history: International review of history education, Vol. 2.* New York, NY: Routledge Falmer.

Wagner, T. (2012a). *Creating innovators: The making of young people who will change the world.* New York, NY: Simon & Schuster.

Wagner, T. (2012b, Saturday/Sunday April 14/15). Educating the next Steve Jobs. *Wall Street Journal,* p. C2.

Wallis, C. (2017, July 26). To err is human—and a powerful prelude to learning. *The Hechinger Report.* Retrieved from hechingerreport.org/getting-errors-all-wrong/

Watanabe, T. (2002). Learning from Japanese Lesson Study. *Educational Leadership, 59*(6), 36–39.

Weber, S., & Mitchell, C. (1995). *That's funny you don't look like a teacher! Interrogating images, identity, and popular culture.* New York, NY: Routledge.

Wells, G., & Chang-Wells, G. L. (1992). *Constructing knowledge together: Classrooms as centers of inquiry and literacy.* Portsmouth, NH: Heinemann.

Wertsch, J. V. (2002). *Voices of collective remembering.* New York, NY: Cambridge University Press.

Whitehead, A. N. (1929). *The aims of education and other essays.* New York, NY: Free Press.

Wideen, M., Mayer-Smith, J., & Moon, B. (1998). A critical analysis of the research on learning to teach: Making the case for an ecological perspective on inquiry. *Review of Educational Research, 68*(2), 130–178.

Wiggins, G., & McTighe, J. (2005). *Understanding by design* (2nd ed.). Washington, DC: Association for Supervision and Curriculum Development.

Winne, P. H., & Azevedo, R. (2014). Metacognition. In R. K. Sawyer (Ed.), *Cambridge handbook of the learning sciences* (2nd ed., pp. 63–87). New York, NY: Cambridge University Press.

Xin, Y. P., Tzur, R., Hord, C., Liu, J., Park, J. Y., & Si, L. (2017). An intelligent tutor-assisted mathematics intervention program for students with learning disabilities. *Learning Disability Quarterly, 40,* 4–16.

Yinger, R. J. (1987, April). *By the seat of your pants: An inquiry into improvisation and teaching.* Paper presented at the annual meeting of the American Educational Research Association, Washington, DC.

Index

SUBJECTS

About the Author

Keith Sawyer is the Morgan Distinguished Professor in Educational Innovations at the University of North Carolina at Chapel Hill. He is one of the world's leading scientific experts on creativity and learning. He has edited or authored 16 books, including a textbook overview of creativity research, *Explaining Creativity: The Science of Human Innovation* (2nd ed., Oxford University Press, 2012), and an influential handbook on scientific studies of learning, *The Cambridge Handbook of the Learning Sciences* (2nd ed., Cambridge University Press. 2014). He has published over 100 scientific articles.

He combines this scientific expertise with a strong hands-on background in real-world creativity. After receiving his computer science degree from MIT in 1982, he began his career with a 2-year stint designing videogames for Atari. He has been a jazz pianist for over 30 years, and spent several years playing piano with Chicago improvisational theater groups, while working towards his PhD in psychology from the University of Chicago. In his current research, he is studying teaching and learning in professional schools of art and design.

Printed and bound by CPI Group (UK) Ltd, Croydon, CR0 4YY

09/06/2025

14685933-0001